Nicolo Paganini

Paganini

Nicolo Paganini

With an Analysis of His Compositions and a Sketch of the History of the Violin

François-Joseph Fétis

New Introduction by
Stewart Pollens

Dover Publications, Inc.
Mineola, New York

Bibliographical Note

This Dover edition, first published in 2013, is an unabridged republication of the work originally published by Schott & Company, London, in 1860. Stewart Pollens has prepared a new Introduction specially for this Dover edition.

Library of Congress Cataloging-in-Publication Data

Fétis, François-Joseph, 1784–1871.
[Notice biographique sur Nicolo Paganini. English]
Nicolo Paganini : with an analysis of his compositions and a sketch of the history of the violin / François-Joseph Fétis ; new introduction by Stewart Pollens.
p. cm.
"Unabridged republication of the work originally published by Schott & Company, London, in 1860."
ISBN-13: 978-0-486-49798-3
ISBN-10: 0-486-49798-4
1. Paganini, Nicoló, 1782–1840. 2. Violinists—Italy—Biography. 3. Violin—History. I. Title.

ML418.P2F32 2013
787.092—dc23

Manufactured in the United States by Courier Corporation
49798401
www.doverpublications.com

INTRODUCTION

THE author of *Nicolo Paganini*, François-Joseph Fétis, was born in Liège, Belgium in 1784 and died in Brussels in 1871. He began his musical education with his father, Antoine, who was a church organist, violinist, and conductor, and from him François-Joseph learned to play the organ, piano, and violin. At the age of nine he tried his hand at composition and wrote a violin concerto, and by the time he entered the Paris Conservatoire in the year 1800 he had composed two piano concertos and three string quartets. There he studied theory and music history and won a second prize in composition in 1807. He married in 1806 and left Paris with his wife in 1811, settling first in Bouvignes and later Douai, where he taught and worked as a church organist. In 1818 he returned to Paris where he continued teaching and composing (his works include seven comic and dramatic operas, a sacred mass and secular cantata, chamber music, and solo works for piano and organ). In 1821 he received a teaching appointment at the Paris Conservatoire and also worked as the Conservatoire's librarian from 1826 through 1830. In 1827 he founded the musicological journal *Revue musicale.*

In 1833 Fétis returned to his native Belgium to become the director of the Brussels Conservatoire. In addition to his administrative duties, he contributed articles and reviews to newspapers and musical journals, and wrote numerous methods, treatises, and manuals devoted to harmony, counterpoint, solfège, accompaniment, and composition. Perhaps his most ambitious undertaking was his *Biographie universelle des musiciens et bibliographie générale de la musique,* a multi-volume work published between 1835 and 1844. This comprehensive musical encyclopedia went through numerous editions; the last, published in 1878–1880, was reprinted as recently as 1963. Though Fétis' *Biographie universelle* has come under sharp criticism for factual errors, it remains an invaluable reference work, particularly with regard to events he witnessed and those he knew personally.

Several of the articles in the *Biographie universelle* were later adapted for republication as monographs, including this one devoted to Nicolo Paganini (with preliminary essays on the history of the violin and violin performance), published in Paris in 1851, and another on Stradivari (with essays on the origin of bowed instruments, the schools of violin making, and a biography of François-Xavier Tourte with a technical study of his bows) published in Paris in 1856. The Paganini monograph was translated into English and published by Schott & Co. in London in 1852, though the Stradivari monograph did not appear in English until 1864. The publication of these monographs coincided with the release of new editions of Paganini's first and second violin concertos and a number of his introductions and variations for violin.

Fétis' opening "Sketch on the History of the Violin" begins with the assertion that bowing was an invention of the West, a point disputed by today's historians, who trace bowing back to tenth-century central Asia. Regarding the earliest known violin, he cites Jean-Benjamin de La Borde's *Essay sur la Musique* (Paris, 1780), which describes a four-string violin labeled "Joann. Kerlino, anno 1449." Fétis remarks that this instrument found its way to Paris and in 1804 was in the hands of the violin maker Jean Gabriel Koliker (active in Paris, 1783–1820). Today, Kerlino is believed to have been a fictional character and the instrument in question either a fabrication by Koliker or perhaps a conversion from an earlier form, such as a viol or lira. Fétis also describes a violin ostensibly by Gaspard Duiffoprugcar bearing the date 1539, though the authenticity of that instrument has also been called into question.

Fétis makes reference to a brother of Andrea Amati named Nicolo, who is said to have assisted in the construction of instruments for Charles IX of France. This information was likely drawn from J. B. Roquefort's *Magasin encyclopédique* (Paris, 1812) or perhaps from M. L'Abbé Sibire's *La chélonomie ou le parfait luthier* (Paris, 1823), though later research in the archives of Cremona by Carlo Bonnetti published in *La Genealogio degli Amati liutai e il primate della scuola liutistica cremonese* (Cremona, 1938) and more recent research efforts reported by Carlo Chiesa in *Andrea Amati opera omnia: les violins du roi* (Cremona, 2007) have failed to reveal the names of any immediate family members of Andrea Amati other than that of his father, Gottardo, and two sons Antonio and Girolamo. One reason for the paltry genealogical information about early members of the Amati family is the lack of relevant census returns from the first half of the sixteenth century and reliance upon sporadic notarial documents. Unfortunately, a number of the labels in the extant Andrea Amati instruments are inauthentic (such as the label in the "Kurtz" Amati violin in the Metropolitan Museum of Art), and it is possible that the lost original labels may have borne the names of both Andrea and Nicolo.

Fétis indicates that Antonio Stradivari was born in 1664 (he was actually born about twenty years earlier) and died in 1747 (1737 is the correct year). He then turns to the Guarneri family, writing that it "was originally from Cremona, and constantly resided there, with the exception of Pietro Guarneri, who settled in Mantua, and still resided there in 1717" (he died there in 1720). However, Andrea Guarneri, the founder of the family of violin makers, was actually born outside of Cremona in the little town of Casalbuttano. Pietro Guarneri, now known as "Peter of Mantua," was not the only member of the family to leave Cremona; there was also his nephew, another Pietro, who settled in Venice and is today known as "Peter of Venice."

Fétis praises Lorenzo Guadagnini's violins and characterizes the instruments of his son Giovanni Battista Guadagnini as "less sought after"—an interesting reversal of fortune, as recent archival research has revealed Lorenzo to have been an innkeeper rather than a violin maker (thereby placing violins bearing his label in limbo) while G.B.'s violins are valued at well over a million dollars.

Jacob Stainer's birth year is given as 1620, whereas 1618-1619 is a better estimate. Other facts about Stainer must also be called into question, such as his alleged apprenticeship with the Amatis, as well as his collaboration with a brother named Marcus, members of the Klotz family, and Albani. Fétis states that Stainer made sixteen instruments that he presented to the emperor and electors of the Holy Roman Empire, but the whereabouts of these instruments are unknown and recent research has yielded no documentary evidence of these supposed gifts. It is important to keep in mind that this historical essay was written before the publication of comparatively well-researched biographical dictionaries of violin makers, such as Willibald Leo Freiherrn von Lütgendorff's *Die Geigen—und Lautenmacher vom Mittelalter bis zur Gegenwart* (Frankfurt, 1904). Previously, historical information about violin makers had been deduced by dealers, who reconstructed birth, death, and dates of activity from authentic violin labels (which were formerly in greater abundance than they are today).

With regard to nineteenth-century violin makers, the facts presented by Fétis are more reliable; Nicolas Lupot's arrival in Paris from Orléans in 1794 is properly noted, and Fétis describes the interesting experimental work carried out by François Chanot, Felix Savart, and J. B. Vuillaume, citing a little-known pamphlet by F. Antolini entitled *Osservazzioni su due Violini esposti nelle sale dell' I.R. Palazzo di Brera uno de' quali di forma non commune* (Milan, 1832).

Fétis' next essay, entitled "Art and Artists," provides a concise review of the history of violin performance, listing the names of early players drawn from such sources as Sylvestro di Ganassi del Fontego's *Regola rubertina* (Venice, 1542) and Marin Mersenne's *Harmonie universelle* (Paris, 1636). He works his way through the Italian school with short biographies of Bassani, Corelli, Tartini, Geminiani, Locatelli, Pugnani, and Viotti, and includes more elaborate entries about the great figures of the French school, including Leclair, Rode, Kreutzer, Baillot, and Lafont, as well as the Belgians De Bériot and Vieuxtemps. German and Bohemian violinists, among them Graun, Konieseck, Benda, Stamitz, and Spohr, are also profiled.

Fétis' remarks about Louis Spohr provide the lead-in for his biography of Paganini, as he notes that Paganini had heard Spohr play and that he "spoke of him in unqualified terms of approbation." Not only did Fétis hear Paganini play and publish reviews of his concerts, but he became a friend and confidant of the virtuoso. When a Parisian newspaper accused Paganini of refusing to play at a charity ball, Fétis helped him draft a letter to the editor refuting these charges and offering the proceeds of another concert to benefit the poor. Fétis also assisted Paganini in composing a lengthy rebuttal in response to rumors that he had been imprisoned for eight years for murdering a mistress. No mention is made in this joint literary effort, which was published in Fétis' own *Revue musicale*, of the fact that Paganini had been jailed for nine days in 1815 on charges of kidnapping and rape, and that his alleged victim nearly died after ingesting a mysterious powder administered by him. Upon Paganini's departure for Genoa in 1834, he wrote to Fétis, "tendering my most affectionate acknowledgements for all the interest and friendship you have shown me . . . I hope you will drop me a line in reply to Genoa, where I am going in order to regain my health." (Translation from G. I .C. de Courcy, *Paganini the Genoese*; Oklahoma, 1957)."

Fétis' initial biographical effort regarding Paganini appeared a year after the violinist's death in the first edition of the *Biographie universelle* (Paganini died on May 27, 1840; the volume with Paganini's biography was published in 1841). Despite their acquaintance, much of the historical information in this entry was drawn from J. M. Schottky's *Paganini's Leben und Treiben als Kunstler und als Mensch* (Prague, 1830), an entry in Gustav Schilling's *Musiklexicon* (1835), and an autobiographical essay, published in the Leipzig *Allgemeine Musikalische Zeitung* in 1830 (which also appeared in French translation in Fétis' *Revue musicale*). This Dover edition is a reprint of the undated second edition of the English version of Fétis' Paganini monograph, which incorporates corrections and drew additional material from other studies, principally Giancarlo Conestabile's *Vita di Niccolò Paganini da Genova* (Perugia, 1851) and Georg Harry's (Paganini's secretary) *Paganini in seinem Reisewagen und Zimmer, in seinem redseligen Stunden, in gesellshaftlichen Zirkeln und seinen Konzerten* (Braunschweig, 1830).

In *Paganini the Genoese,* author Geraldine de Courcy excoriates Fétis and characterizes his biography as a "manifestly hastily concocted, historically irresponsible, and professionally unethical piece of hack work that has contributed, and to no small degree, to the numerous inaccuracies, inconsistencies, and confusion of the Paganini epic ever since." However, she cites few errors and turns to Fétis' monograph for information, praises his "impartial" concert reviews, and summarizes his account of Paganini's Turin concerts as "concise and manifestly correct." One major point of contention, which she repeatedly brings up, concerns Fétis' "deliberately injected preposterous fairy tale of the Tuscan 'grand dame'," which he recounts as follows:

> "Although he was still in the prime of youth, Paganini knew of nothing but success and profit, when, during one of those hallucinations to which all great artists are subject, the Violin lost its attractions in his eyes. A lady of rank having fallen desperately in love with him, and the feeling being reciprocated, he withdrew with her to an estate she possessed in Tuscany. This lady played the Guitar, and Paganini imbibed a taste for that instrument and applied himself as sedulously to its practice as he had formerly done with the Violin. He soon discovered new resources, which he imparted to his friend; and during a period of three years, he devoted all the energies of his mind to its study, and to agricultural pursuits, for which the lady's estate afforded him ample opportunities. It was at this period he wrote his two sonatas for Guitar and Violin, which form his second and third works."

Certain details of this anecdote–such as Paganini's fascination with the guitar and the peculiar reference to "agricultural pursuits"–appear in Paganini's two autobiographical sketches, though in a footnote to the passage regarding Paganini's love affair with a "lady of rank" and his withdrawal to her estate, Fétis indicates that this information was related to him directly by Paganini. The violin and guitar sonatas referred to above are presumably Paganini's Opus 2 and Opus 3 (circa 1801–1806), which each consist of six sonatas for violin and guitar, though Opus 2 is dedicated to Signor Dellepiane (a resident of the Tuscan town of Lucca), while Opus 3 is dedicated "to the *regazza* Eleanora," who is identified as Eleanora Quilici (also of Lucca). De Courcy remarks that Eleanora Quilici "was evidently [Paganini's] first love" and points out that she was the only one outside of his family who was provided for in his will. However, Eleanora Quilici came from a humble background and was unlikely to have owned or resided on an estate. This better defines the circumstances of Princess Elise (a sister of Napoleon and certainly a "lady of rank"), who in 1806 appointed Paganini to her newly formed court orchestra in Lucca, a position he held for three years. Surprisingly, de Courcy cites a second-hand account that corroborates Paganini's romantic involvement with Princess Elise, so Fétis' allusion to this affair can scarcely be characterized as "preposterous."

Nevertheless, those requiring the last word in historical accuracy should consult the writings of modern scholars, such as de Courcy, who have scoured the collected letters of Paganini and his correspondents and ascertained the precise dates of his appointments, travels, and concert appearances from official documents, journals, and newspapers. Furthermore, a more thorough listing of Paganini's compositions can be found in modern encyclopedic works such as the *New Grove Dictionary of Music and Musicians* and the online dictionary *Wikipedia.* Despite some factual errors (which for the most part are found in the preliminary essays) and a tendency to romanticize its subject, Fétis' *Biographical Notice of Nicolo Paganini* remains an important historical source. The author's first-hand accounts of Paganini's playing, personal habits, and social behavior are not only entertaining but provide an added dimension to this colorful portrait of a legendary virtuoso.

STEWART POLLENS

Index.

Illustrations.

SKETCH OF THE

HISTORY OF THE VIOLIN.

The Instrument.

DESPITE all contrary assertions, based upon pretended monuments, Oriental, Greek, and Roman antiquity was unacquainted with instruments played with a bow. Neither India nor Egypt furnish the least traces of them; nor do Greece and Italy; nor, in fact, does the whole of the old civilized world. As I stated in the "Résumé Philosophique de l'Histoire de la Musique," the bow comes from the West; it was introduced into the whole of Europe by the western nations. Though Viols are found among the modern Arabs in Persia and Turkey, they were taken there by Europeans in the time of the Crusades. The Goudock of the Russian peasant, and the Crwth of the ancient Irish, appear to proceed from the highest antiquity, and to have been the type of instruments of this nature. The Irish chroniclers speak of musicians who, in the sixth century, were celebrated for their talent on the Crwth, a species of Viol with six strings; and Venance Fortunat, a Latin poet who wrote in 609, states distinctly that this instrument belonged to Great Britain.

It is not my intention to follow up here the various transformations of bow instruments in the middle ages; it will suffice to observe that there were frequent changes in them from the thirteenth to the sixteenth century; as much in the common kinds, vulgarly called in French Rebec, and in German Geige ohne Bunde (Violins without band or side pieces), which possessed only three strings, as in the improved Viols, the body of which was formed of belly and back joined by side pieces, as in our Violins, Tenors, and Basses. The smaller kinds also possessed only three strings; the larger kind had four; there were also others with five, six, and seven strings.

In the middle ages, the Rebec, called Rubebbe, possessed but two strings. It is the same instrument which in Arabia acquired the name of Rebab. From the fifteenth century it is found with its three strings. This instrument took nearly the form of a mandoline; the neck and the body being formed of a single piece, the finger-board being as wide as the entire instrument, and reaching within a short distance of the bridge. No passage was left for the bow in the body of the instrument, but the body was very narrow, and the bridge formed a point for the middle string to rest upon, so that this string could be touched by the bow without touching the others. Like all instruments later than the fifteenth century, the Rebec was made of four different sizes, the smallest of which was called Discant, or upper; then followed, in progressively larger proportions, the Alto, the Tenor, and the Bass. The dancing-master's Kit, of the latter years of the eighteenth century, was all that remained of the ancient Rebec.

The Viol was called Vielle in the middle ages. This is the Viola of the Italians, and the Vihuela of the Spaniards. There were several kinds. As early as the fifteenth century, one of this kind had a flat belly, and a place for fixing the strings similar to that of the Guitar. As in the Lute, and all stringed instruments played with the fingers, the finger-board was divided into distances for placing the fingers. From the fifteenth century the bellies of Viols assumed the raised or vaulted form, the backs remaining flat. The cavities at the side, which had formerly been very large and straight, were made in the shape of a section of a circle, and were reduced to the dimensions necessary for the use of the bow. The raised bellies rendered it necessary to alter the bridge into the bridge-shape, so as to incline towards the ribs. Hence the term Bridge, which is called by the Italians, from its form, Ponticello. The divisions for the fingers on the finger-board were retained on the Viols up to the second half of the seventeenth century. During the fifteenth century the vaulted form of Viol possessed five strings; in the commencement of the sixteenth it had six. The first string was called in Italy Canto, the second Sotana, the third Mezzana, the fourth Tenore, the fifth Bordone, and the sixth Basso.

The Viol was divided into three kinds, which were called Upper or Soprano, Tenor, and Bass. The Tenor was used also for playing the second upper part, or Alto; it was then tuned a note higher: the tuning of the upper Viol was, commencing from the first string, D, A, E, C, G, D; that of the Tenor tuned to Alto, A, E, B, G, D, A; the same instrument tuned to Tenor, G, D, A, F, C, G; and the Bass, D, A, E, C, G, D. At the commencement of the seventeenth century, the use of instruments specially for accompanying the voice became general; there was added to the other Viols a Double-Bass Viol, which was called Violone, that is, large Viol. This also had six strings, and was tuned a fourth lower than the Bass Viol, thus A, E, B, G, D, A. Prior to 1650, this instrument was rarely used in France, it was then called "Viole à la mode de Lorraine."

In imitation of the vaulted form of Viol, there was made, already in the fifteenth century, a small instrument of the same kind, which the Italians called Violino, that is, small Viol. This is the instrument which was called Violon in France, and Geige in Germany.

It is probable that the Violin originally had the same number of strings as the other Viols; that these were tuned a fourth above the upper Viol, viz., G, D, A, F, C, G; and that the neck also possessed divisions for the fingers; but it was soon discovered that the finger-board of the Violin was not wide enough to allow any one to play with facility on so large a number of strings; and that the space for the fingers to produce the notes was too narrow to admit of divisions. These were removed; the strings, reduced to four, were tuned in fifths; making the first string E, as it is at the present day. It cannot be doubted that these improvements originated in France; for on reference to the list of instruments employed in the "Orfeo" of Monteverde, it will be seen that the Violin was called in Italy, at the end of the sixteenth century, and the beginning of the seventeenth, "Violino piccolo alla francese."

The oldest maker of Violins on record was a native of Brittany, named Jean Kerlin. He followed his trade about the middle of the fifteenth century. La Borde, author of the imperfect and voluminous "Essai sur la Musique," relates that he saw in Brittany a Violin with four strings, the neck of which did not appear to have been changed, and which, instead of the ordinary tail-piece, had a small piece of ivory inlaid, pierced with four holes. This Violin was thus labelled, "Joann. Kerlino, anno 1449." It was afterwards brought to Paris, and Koliker, a musical instrument maker of that city, had it in his possession in 1804. The belly was more raised than in good modern Italian Violins, and was not equally rounded at the upper and lower extemities; the sides were ill-formed and flattened. Its tone was sweet and muffled, and resembled that of instruments made by Antonio Amati at the close of the sixteenth century. After Jean Kerlin, there is a lapse of sixty years in the history of the manufacture of Violins, for the only maker of this instrument whose name has come down to us is Gaspard Duiffoprugcar, born in the Italian Tyrol, who commenced making his Violins at Bologna about 1510, working afterwards in Paris, and at Lyons. One Violin only of the large pattern which bears his name is in existence; it is dated 1539. The quality of tone of this instrument is powerful and penetrating, but when played upon for some time, it loses its intensity. Like an old man, it needs repose to recover its faculties. The scroll represents the head of a king's jester, with a plaited frill. This Violin belonged to M. Meerts, formerly first solo violinist of the Theatre Royal, Brussels, and professor at the Conservatory of that city.

Gaspard di Salo, thus called from being born in the small town of Salo, on the lake of Garda, in Lombardy, worked in the second half of the sixteenth century. He was specially celebrated for his Viols, Basses, and Double-Bass Viols, then more used than the Violin. Nevertheless, an excellent Violin of his make, dated 1576, was met with in a collection of valuable instruments which were sold at Milan in 1807; and the Baron de Bagge was in possession of one of which Rodolphe Kreutzer often spoke with admiration. These instruments, of rather a large pattern, possess a powerful tone, approximating to that of the Alto.

Contemporaneously with Gaspard di Salo, the two brothers, Andrea and Nicolo Amati became famous for the excellence of their Viols and Bass Viols; they also made excellent Violins, the tone of which was mellow and agreeable, but they were wanting in power, like all the instruments made by the members of this family. Andrea and Nicolo, about 1570, made Violins of a large pattern for the chamber music of Charles IX. King of France. These instruments were remarkable for the beauty of their form, and perfection of finish. They were covered with an oil varnish, of a golden colour, shaded with red. Two of these were seen in Paris by Professor Cartier about 1810. The successors of Andrea and Nicolo Amati retained in the family the fame of those artists for more than a century and a half. Antonio, son of Andrea, Geronimo, his brother, and Nicolo, son of Geronimo, were instrument makers of high repute, but the sonority of their Violins and Basses, admirably adapted for the music of their time, is much too weak for the modern noisy system; however, Paganini possessed a Violin of Geronimo Amati, of large pattern, which he prized most highly.

Two Italian makers were also famous at the beginning and towards the middle of the seventeenth century for their Violins: the first is Giovanni Paolo Maggini, who had an establishment at Brescia, his native town. His instruments are dated from 1612 to 1640. The pattern of these Violins is generally very large; although there are some of the small size. The bellies are raised, the back, rather flat at the extremities, swells out exceedingly towards the sides, which are very wide; the curves being well rounded towards the angles. A double row of purfling runs round both belly and back, terminating in some instances in an ornament at the upper and lower parts of the back. Most of Maggini's Violins are varnished with spirit of wine, of a deep gold colour. Their tone is less mellow than that of the Stradiuari, and less powerful than the Guarnieri; it has more analogy to the tone of the Viol, and its character is somewhat melancholic. The second maker of that period celebrated in Italy is Giovanni Granzino; he resided at Milan, and worked there from 1612 to 1635. His Violins, of large pattern, resemble those of Gaspard di Salo.

The fame of Italy for the construction of bow instruments attained its zenith between the middle of the seventeenth century and the first half of the eighteenth. To this period belong the names of Stradiuari and Guarnieri. Antonio Stradiuari, better known under the Latinised name of Stradivarius, the most celebrated maker of Violins, Viols, and Basses, was born at Cremona in 1664; he reached his eighty-third year, working until his death in 1747. A pupil of the Amati, he worked a long time with them, and upon their models. Towards 1700 he left them, and from that time changed his proportions, increased his form, lowered the bellies, and was as fastidious in the degrees of thickness of the wood as he was in the choice of the wood he employed. Contrary to the principles of the older Italian masters, his thickness increased towards the centre, in order to give support to the bridge upon which the tension of the strings bears, and diminished gradually towards the sides of the instrument. All is calculated, in the works of this excellent artist, for the better production of tone. To these advantages are superadded equality in all the strings, grace of form, finish of details, and brilliancy of varnish. In a large concert room a good Violin of Giuseppe Guarnieri has more power of sonority; but in a drawing-room nothing can possibly equal the brilliant mellowness of a well-preserved Stradiuari. Unfortunately many have fallen into the hands of unskilful workmen for repairs.

The family of the Guarnieri or Guarnerius has also become illustrious for the manufacture of bow instruments. This family was also originally of Cremona, and constantly resided there, with the exception of Pietro Guarnieri, who settled at Mantua, and still resided there in 1717. The most celebrated of these makers is Giuseppe Guarnieri, called in Italy "Guarnieri del Gesu," from his

Violins bearing the mark IHS. He was born at Cremona at the close of the seventeenth century. It is said that he learned his trade in the workshop of Stradiuari, but he never attained his master's delicacy of finish; on the contrary, his work evinces very frequently great carelessness. His sound-holes, nearly straight and angular, are badly shaped; his purfling badly traced; in fact, his instruments carry no masterly appearance, and one is tempted to believe that the excellent quality of their tone arises more from the happy choice of material than from studied principles. Nevertheless, on close inspection, it is evident positive principles guided him in the construction of his instruments; he has copied no maker who preceded him. He had two patterns, one small, the other large. The instruments of small pattern are the most numerous, their bellies are slightly raised, and their thickness rather exceeds that of the Stradiuari. The large patterns which proceed from Giuseppe Guarnieri are few in number, and rarely met with. It was upon one of these Violins that Paganini played at all his concerts. The tone of these instruments is exceedingly brilliant, and carries to a great distance, but is less round and mellow than the instruments of Stradiuari, and pleases less near than at a certain distance.

After Stradiuari and Giuseppe Guarnieri, the art seems to have remained at its highest point of excellence, and the Italian makers appear not to have sought to improve, contenting themselves with copying the one or the other of these masters. Lorenzo Guadagnini, a pupil of Stradiuari, copied the small pattern of his master. The first and second string of his Violins possess brilliancy and roundness, but the third is unfortunately muffled. He had a son, who worked at Milan until towards the end of 1770, following the style of his father; but his instruments are less sought after. The Gagliani also copied the Stradiuari, but their instruments are far from equalling those of the master, doubtless from want of care in the selection of material. Ruggieri and Alvani copied the form of Giuseppe Guarnieri; they produced good Violins, which are less valuable, however, than the Stradiuari.

The Tyrol lays claim to some excellent makers of bow instruments, the chief of whom is Jacob Stainer, who was born about 1620, at Absom, a village near Inspruck. This celebrated maker, at three different periods, changed his make. Firstly, while pupil of the Amati of Cremona: the Violins of this period are admirably finished, and are extremely scarce. The belly is more raised than in the Amati, the scrolls longer and wider in the lower part. All the labels of these Violins are written and signed in his own handwriting. One of these magnificent instruments, dated 1644, was the property of Gardel, ballet-master of the Opera at Paris, who performed upon it successfully in the ballet of "La Dansomanie." Secondly, when established at Absom, after having married, he produced an immense number of instruments carelessly finished, from 1650 to 1667. However, after having led a life of poverty for several years, obliged to hawk his own Violins, which he sold for six florins each, he received orders from some noblemen, which improved his position. His genius from this period took a new flight, and he produced some splendid instruments, which are recognised by scrolls that represent heads of animals, by the close veining of the bellies, by the close and even small ribs, and by the varnish, resembling red mahogany faded by time into a brown colour. Stainer was assisted at this time by his brother Marcus, who later in life entered the order of the Brother Hermits, by the three brothers Klotz (Mathias, George, and Sebastian), and by Albani, all of whom were his pupils. The reproach attached to Stainer's instruments of possessing a nasal tone applies only to this period, the labels of which are printed; there are, however, some admirable instruments of this time, which were in the possession of the violinist Ropiquet, of the Marquis de las Rosas, a grandee of Spain, of the Count de Marp, a Parisian amateur, and of Frey, an artist of the Opera, and publisher of music. There is an excellent Tenor of this period, formerly the property of M. Matrôt de Préville, governor of the port of L'Orient.

The third period of Stainer's career commences from his retiring into a convent after the death of his wife. In the tranquillity of the cloister, he determined to close his artistic life by the production of *chefs-d'œuvre.* Having obtained some wood of the first quality through the medium of his superior, he made sixteen Violins—models, combining every perfection; sent one to each of the twelve chiefs of electorates of the Empire, and presented the remaining four to the Emperor. Since then, these instruments are known under the name of Stainer-électeurs. Their tone is pure, metallic, and aerial, like the beautiful voice of a woman; they are graceful and elegant in form, exquisitely finished in all the details, and have a transparent varnish of a gold colour; such are the qualities which distinguish these productions of the third and last period of Stainer's talent. The labels are in the hand-writing of this celebrated maker. Three of these rare instruments only are now to be met with; the fate of the others remains unknown. The first was given by the Empress Maria Theresa to Kennis, a Belgian violinist from Liège, after whose death it was taken to England, and became the property of Sir Richard Betenson, Bart. Another Stainer-électeur was purchased in Germany in 1771 by the Duke of Orleans, grandfather of King Louis Philippe, for the sum of 3,500 florins. Afterwards, this prince, having discontinued playing the Violin, gave it to the younger Novoigille, in token of the pleasure he experienced in hearing him accompany Madame de Montesson. This precious Violin became the property of the violinist Cartier in 1817; it was in the hands of this artist when I heard and saw it. The third Violin Elector was in the possession of the King of Prussia, Frederick William II.

After leaving Stainer, the Klotz family copied his models of the second period, and these instruments are not unfrequently mistaken for those of the master; they are, however, readily distinguished by the varnish; that of Klotz, instead of a deep red, has a black ground shaded with yellow; the tone of Mathias Klotz' instruments is silvery, but of little power. These artists produced many pupils in the Tyrol, who imitated the Cremona models; but these imitations are easily discoverable by the inferior quality of the wood, the varnish, which is very dark, and the tone, which is deficient in every quality.

The ancient manufacture of musical instruments in France, incontestably inferior to that of Italy, is represented, during the reigns of Henry the Fourth and Louis the Thirteenth, by Jacques Bocquay, born at Lyons, who settled in Paris; Pierret, his townsman, who produced more instruments, but of inferior finish; Antoine Despons, and Adrien Véron; these makers generally copied Amati. The Violins of the successor of Bocquay, Guersan, his pupil, are of small pattern, and finely finished. They have become extremely scarce; it is supposed that there are not more than twenty which can be considered as his own make; these are varnished in oil. The others were made in his workshop by his pupils; they are of inferior quality, and varnished in spirits of wine. The contemporaries of Guersan at Paris were Castagnery and Saint-Paul, whose Violins were formerly esteemed for accompaniment. After these came Salomon, whose instruments rivalled those of Guersan. Towards the end of the reign of Louis the Fourteenth, Lagetto enjoyed a certain reputation. As regards the ancient manufacture in the provinces of France, there is nothing which rises above mediocrity, with the exception of Médard, a contemporary of Geronimo Amati, whose models he copied. He lived at Nancy at the commencement of the seventeenth century. Lambert, surnamed "Charpentier de la Lutherie," lived a century later in the same town. He produced nothing of any note. Saunier, his pupil, surpassed his master in finish; but in general Lorraine was the country of industry, not art.

In the modern manufacture of instruments at Paris, Finth is specially distinguished. He was a German, who worked about 1770, and followed the proportions of Stradiuari; all his Violins, varnished in oil, are finished with care. They were greatly sought after in the first instance, but a change of taste followed, and opinion fell into a contrary excess. After Finth came Picte, a pupil of Saunier, whose Violins were given as prizes to the pupils of the Conservatory of Paris, at the beginning of the present century; they have been esteemed of little value. Not so with Lupot, who came from Orleans to settle in Paris in 1794. He studied, with great perseverance, the proportions of Stradiuari, incontestably the best, and selected the finest wood that could be obtained. Lupot made the manufacture of Violins his great study, and their finish a work of love. They are highly esteemed, and stand next in value with artists to good Cremona instruments.

Thus far we have only seen the manufacture of bow instruments cultivated by inspiration or by imitation; science was not brought to bear as an element in the construction of these instruments; but we have arrived at a period of transition in this respect, less perhaps, from the results obtained, than from the foundations which have been laid: and I will first advert to the several essays which have been made with the view of dispensing with certain portions of the instrument, considered as obstacles to the free production of vibration.

The first essay of this kind was made in 1816 by François Chanot, the son of an instrument-maker of Mirecourt, afterwards an engineer in the navy. Convinced that the best means of producing vibration in all the various parts of the Violin was to preserve, as far as it was practicable, the fibres of the wood lengthwise, he concluded that the shoulders of the ordinary Violin, with their angles, were insuperable obstacles to a free and powerful quality of tone; he believed, also, that the hollowing out of the belly to give it the vaulted form was contrary to theoretical principles, and consequently a radical error. He was persuaded, moreover, that short fibres favoured the production of acute tones, and long fibres grave ones. Upon these principles he constructed a Violin, the belly of which was only slightly raised, the sound-holes nearly straight, and, in place of sloping the instrument after the ordinary form, he depressed the sides gradually, similar to the body of a Guitar. With a view of favouring as much as possible the vibration of the belly, he attached the strings to the lower part of it, instead of to the ordinary tail-piece. This done, Chanot submitted his Violin to the Academies of Sciences and Fine Arts of the French Institute, and a favourable report of the essay was published in the "Moniteur Universel" on the 22nd of August, 1817. The judgment pronounced by these institutions has not been confirmed by the opinion of artists.

It is to be remarked, that what Chanot conceived to be a discovery was simply returning to the form of Viols of the middle ages; that the form had been adopted by able makers, and that there is still extant a Bass Viol of Gaspard di Salo, the angles of which are removed, in the possession of M. Frazzini at Milan; that another Bass of the same form, constructed by Pietro Guarnieri, belongs to M. Cappi at Mantua; and that M. de Rovetta of Bergamo, possesses an old Violin of the same form. The artists who made these essays discovered that the results did not answer their expectations.

A retired officer of the Italian army, M. Galbussera, reproduced the pretended invention of Chanot in a Violin which he exhibited in the Palace of Brera at Milan in 1832. M. Antolini, of that city, a distinguished artist, criticised in a small pamphlet the false principle which led to this return to primitive forms.*

Some years after Chanot's Violin had been consigned to the department of the museum specially devoted to this object, Felix Savart, a physicist of eminence, struck with the discoveries of Chladni on the communication of vibrations and regularity of sonorous waves, devoted himself with great ardour to the application of these discoveries in the construction of bow instruments, and after several experiments, made with great sagacity, he arrived at the following deductions:—1st, When two or a larger number of bodies, whatever they may be, come into immediate contact, and one is directly put into motion, they all produce the same number of vibrations at the same time; 2nd, All these vibrations follow parallel directions; 3rd, The increase of the sound of any kind of body—for example of a string—depends upon the simultaneity of the vibrations of the bodies with which this string is in contact; and this increase is carried to its highest point when the bodies put into motion by communication are in such conditions that, if they were directly put into motion, they would produce the same number of vibrations as the body acted upon in the first instance.

* "Osservazzioni su due Violini esposti nelle sale dell' I. R. Palazzo di Brera uno de' quali di forma non commune." Milan, 1832, in 8vo.

The chief consequences of these principles are, that the vibrations produced by the strings of the Violin are communicated to the belly by the bridge, from the belly to the back by the sounding-post; and that the oscillations, in equal number, of all these bodies, cause equal vibration, and, by similar numbers of oscillations, to the mass of air held in suspension within the body of the instrument; hence it follows that the object in the construction of this sonorous box is to favour as much as possible the communication of the sound-waves, and to bring them into harmony. In seeking the application of this theory to the manufacture of bow instruments, Savart fell into error in the first pamphlet he wrote upon this subject,* when he expressed the opinion that the curves, the angles, and the raised belly adopted by the old manufacturers could only have proceeded from the prejudices of routine; but he discovered this error while prosecuting the continuation of his studies, and he ultimately extolled the proportions of Stradiuari, which he first believed to be only favourable to good effects from considerations which the celebrated maker had not perceived.

A manufacturer of the greatest intelligence, M. Vuillaume, sen., born at Mirecourt, and settled in Paris, devoted himself to the principles of constructing bow instruments, at the very time Savart was occupied in endeavouring to discover them. These two ingenious men, in constant communication with each other on this subject, reciprocally aided each other. The artist brought to the man of science the tribute of his experience, and the man of science to the artist the result of his meditations. Vuillaume had been for a lengthened period engaged in experiments on the density, homogeneity, and the elasticity of various woods, convinced of the importance of this matter for the solution of most of the problems of acoustics relative to the sonorous quality of instruments. He was thus enabled to discover the most suitable wood to be used in the repairing of ancient instruments, as regards their quality or their defects, and the most signal success

* "Mémoire sur la construction des instruments à cordes et à archet, lu à l'Academie des Sciences le 31 Mai, 1819." Paris: Déterville. One vol. in 8vo.

crowned his researches. Many instruments of great price, after having been deteriorated by unskilful hands, recovered their former value through the ability of this distinguished maker. What he acquired in this respect, he applied to all instruments of his own manufacture, and his deep study of the proportions of the best ancient instruments, joined to his knowledge of the special nature of woods, and the laws of vibration, has enabled him to produce a multitude of very superior instruments, which require only time to be stamped with excellence.

It will be seen, from what has been said, that the art of constructing bow instruments has departed from the prejudices of routine, working in the dark, and by imitation, to pursue the wake of science, of observation, and of calculation. There can be no doubt that this is a real progress; but to shield this progress from all contestation, the effect of time is requisite. To bring a good instrument to that state of equilibrium which will make its qualities manifest, on the one hand it is necessary that the materials employed in its construction should, for a lengthened period, be submitted to the action of the various states of temperature and atmosphere; and on the other, that the elasticity of its various parts should have been put for a long time into action, to acquire all its development.

Art and Artists.

WHEN singers possessed only part-songs, such as madrigals, and glees for four, five, or six voices, positive instrumental music was unknown. Instrumentalists played the voice parts in unison, either on bow instruments, or the Organ and Spinett, or on wind instruments, such as Oboes, Flutes, Horns, or Cromorns; for each instrument was then divided into upper, high, counter, tenor, and bass. The ricercari and dance tunes for four, five, or six Viols, formed the only instrumental music properly so called. Little skill was necessary in the execution, and artists required no greater amount of talent than the music itself displayed. As regards the Violin, few persons then cultivated it. In Italy one Giovanni Battista, surnamed Del Violino, is constantly cited, on account of his Violin performance. He lived in 1590. As regards Giulio Tiburtino and Ludovico Lasagrino, who were in high repute at Florence about 1540, and of whom Ganassi del Fontego speaks in his "Regola Rubertina," they were performers on the Viol, and not Violinists. The same may be said of Beaulieu, Salmon, and others, who were at the court of France. According to Mersenne, the French distinguished themselves as violinists at the commencement of the seventeenth century. He speaks in terms of great praise of the elegant playing of Constantine, King of the Violins; of the vehement enthusiasm of Boccan; of the delicacy and expression of Lazarin and Foucard. These artists lived in 1630. However, France soon afterwards lost its superiority in that respect. In 1650, Father Castrovillari, a monk of Padua, became distinguished by his performance on the Violin, and by the music he wrote for that instrument. The art of executing difficulties upon it must have attained a high degree of progress in the north of

Europe, even as far back as 1675, for Jean Jacques Walther, principal Violin soloist at the court of Saxony, published at this period several works, among which one is peculiarly remarkable, and bears for its title "Hortulus Chelicus" (Mayence, 1688, in oblong quarto of 129 pages), containing sonatas and serenades, to be performed on a single Violin, with double, triple, and quadruple strings. This work, which displays great invention, consists of twenty-four pieces. The title of the last may serve to show the novelties which Walther introduced to the art of playing the Violin: "Serenade for a chorus of Violins, Trembling Organ, small Guitar, Bagpipe, two Trumpets and Kettle Drums, German Lyre, and Muted Harp, for a single Violin." The various effects of this piece for a single Violin prove that Walther was the Paganini of his day.

Giovanni Battista Bassani, a Venetian composer, was a pupil of Castrovillari for the Violin, and became celebrated for the excellent style of his instrumental music. Among many other compositions of various styles, there is a set of his sonatas "da camera" for Violin and Bass, published in 1679, and thirteen sonatas for two Violins and Bass, excellent of their kind, and which fixed the style of music for bow instruments at the period at which they appeared. Bassani had the honour of being the master of Corelli, the great artist, possessed of immense talent, who by the elevation of his ideas, and the perfection of his style, placed himself at the head of the Violin School, and hastened the progress of the art considerably. Arcangelo Corelli, a name justly celebrated in the annals of music, will descend to ages unborn without losing a particle of its glory, whatever revolutions may be effected in the domains of art. The great artist who bore that name, no less celebrated for his compositions than for his marvellous execution at that period, was born in 1653, at Fusignano, a small town in the States of the Church, and died at Rome, on the 18th of January, 1713. His contemporaries were not jealous of his glory, for the whole of Europe welcomed his talent with unanimous acclamations; his countrymen deposited his remains in the Pantheon, and erected a monument to him close to that of Raphael. At the expiration of a century and a half, Corelli is still considered as the primitive type of the best Violin schools; and although the art has been enriched by many effects unknown in his day; although its mechanism has attained a high degree of perfection, the study of his works is still one of the best for the acquirement of a broad and majestic style. His fifth work, composed of twelve sonatas for the Violin, with the continued Bass for the Harpsichord, printed at Rome in 1700, is a masterpiece of its kind.

The art of playing the Violin, and the composition of music for this instrument, continued during the whole of the eighteenth century to progress rapidly. At the commencement of this century in almost every town of Italy, a distinguished violinist was met with. The genius of Corelli roused that of every artist. At Pisa, Costantino Clari, equally remarkable as composer and executant; at Florence, Francesco Veracini; at Bologna, Geronimo Laurenti; at Modena, Antonio Vitali; at Massa di Carrara, Cosmo Perelli and Francesco Ciampi; at Lucca, Lombardi; at Cremona, Visconti, whose counsels greatly aided Stradiuari in the manufacture of his instruments; at Pistoia, Giacopino; at Naples, Michaele Mascitti. Others, as Matteo Alberti, Tommaso Albinoni, Carlo Tessarini, and Antonio Vivaldi, all pupils of Corelli, were in their day not only *virtuosi* of the first order, but admirable writers of instrumental music. Vivaldi was one of those predestined artists who impress upon the art of their time a new direction. To him may be attributed the first improvement of the concerto; for the *concerto grosso* of Corelli is a work in which all the parts agree together, and each in turn partakes of its interest. "L'Estro Armonico" of Vivaldi, composed of twelve concertos for four Violins, two Viols, Violoncello, and Thorough-Bass for the Organ, follows this model; but in his sixth, seventh, eighth, ninth, tenth, eleventh and twelfth work, the genius of the author takes another flight, and although there is no division of *solo* and *tutti*, the principal Violin part governs all the rest. The melodies of Vivaldi bear a modern complexion that Somis and Geminiani imitated.

Among the above-mentioned galaxy of distinguished talent,

the model violinist of the first half of the eighteenth century was Giuseppe Tartini, born at Pirano, in Istria, on the 12th of April, 1692. His early days were beset with difficulties, but having had the opportunity of hearing the celebrated violinist, Veracini, who happened to be at Venice when he was there, his vocation revealed itself. He withdrew to Ancona to practise uninterruptedly; and he applied himself in solitude more especially to the fundamental principle of bow movements, principles which have since served as the basis of every Violin school of Italy and of France. Settled in Padua in 1721, as principal soloist and chapel master of the celebrated church of St. Anthony, he passed forty-nine years of peace and comfort, solely occupied with the labours of his art, and died there on the 16th of February, 1770. In 1728, he established a school in that city, which became famous throughout Europe, and from which issued a multitude of violinists, among whom the following may be cited: Nardini, Pasqualino Bini, Alberghi, Domenico Ferrari, to whom is attributed the invention of harmonic sounds, Carminati, Capuzzi, Madame de Sirmen, and the French violinists, Pagin and La Houssaye. Tartini not only contributed towards perfecting the art of playing the Violin by his compositions for that instrument, but by the pupils he formed. His style is generally elevated; his ideas varied, and his harmony pure without being dry. The number of his published concertos and manuscripts amounts to nearly one hundred and fifty. There are also nearly fifty sonatas of his, among which is his "Sonata del Diavolo," the anecdote of which is not dissimilar to that told of Paganini. Tartini thus related it:—"One night in 1713, I dreamt that I had entered into a compact with the devil, who was to be at my service. All succeeded to my utmost desires. My wishes were always anticipated, my desires surpassed, by the services of my new domestic. I thought of giving him my Violin, with the view of discovering whether he would play some fine things upon it; but what was my surprise when I heard a sonata so exquisitely beautiful and original, executed with such consummate skill and intelligence, that my deepest conceptions could not find its parallel.

Overcome with surprise and pleasure, I lost my breath, which violent sensation awoke me. I instantly seized my Violin in the hope of remembering some portion of what I had heard, but in vain. The piece which this dream suggested, and which I wrote at the time, is doubtless the best of all my compositions, and I still call it "Sonata del Diavolo," but it sinks so much into insignificance compared with what I heard, that I would have broken my instrument and abandoned music for ever, had my means permitted me to do so."

Among the pupils of Corelli, one of the most distinguished was Geminiani, who was born at Lucca, about 1680. Having terminated his studies under this celebrated master, he went to England in 1714, made some good pupils there, and died in Dublin, the 17th of September, 1762, in his eighty-third year. His execution was brilliant and solid, but his compositions were wanting in imagination, being only a weak imitation of Vivaldi's style. Somis, another pupil of Corelli, was born in Piedmont, towards the close of the seventeenth century, and had visited Rome and Venice in his youth, for the purpose of learning under the *virtuosi* of that period. Corelli made him study his sonatas, and Somis at first became attached to his style, but when he heard Vivaldi, he modified his style, and copied him in his compositions. Somis was the founder of the Piedmontese Violin school, which, after the death of Tartini, greatly influenced the art of playing upon this instrument. Baptiste Anet, better known as Baptiste, who received lessons from Corelli, came to Paris about 1700, and was considered a prodigy, not at all surprising at a period when, according to Lully, "the best violinists of the opera, and of the king's band, were incapable of playing their parts without previous study." Rather a mediocre musician, Baptiste made but one pupil, Senaillé, so that he effected no improvement in the formation of a French school of violinists. Besides, he resided only five years in Paris, having accepted a position in Poland which was offered to him.

The glory of laying the foundation of a Violin school in France was reserved for Jean Marie Leclair, pupil of Somis, and a celebrated violinist. He was born at Lyons in 1697. He at first used the Violin as a dancing master, for in his youth he appeared as a dancer at Rouen; but having been engaged as ballet-master at Turin, Somis, who was pleased at hearing him play some dance tunes, gave him lessons, by which he made rapid progress. After two years' study, the pupil surpassed the master. Leclair continued his practice perseveringly, and ultimately became a celebrated performer. Arriving in Paris in 1729, he was engaged in the orchestra of the Opera, and afterwards in the king's band. The pupils he formed, and the publication of his sonatas, his duets, and trios, are the starting points of the school of French violinists. Jean Baptiste Senaillé had also some part in influencing the first development of this school. Born in Paris, the 23rd of November, 1687, he took lessons from Queversin, one of the twenty-four violinists of the king's great band, and afterwards became the pupil of Baptiste Anet. The great fame of the Italian violinists of that period induced him to proceed to Modena, where he received lessons from Antonio Vitali. He produced a great sensation in that city, and became attached to the Court, through the influence of the Grand Duchess. Returning to Paris in 1719, he made some excellent pupils, among others Guignon, and probably Guillemain, who obtained a certain degree of celebrity for some admirable sonatas for the Violin.

Of all Corelli's pupils, the one who departed the most from his master's style, and by his daring arrived at most extraordinary results, was Pietro Locatelli, justly celebrated as a violinist, born at Bergamo in 1693. He could have received but few lessons from his illustrious master, being scarcely sixteen years of age when Corelli died. Bold and original, he invented new combinations in tuning the Violin, in double notes, arpeggios, and harmonic sounds. The most important work in which he put forth the result of his discoveries in these various matters, bears the title of "Arte de nuova modulazione." The French editions of this work are entitled "Caprices énigmatiques." If Locatelli, who died in Holland in 1764, did not produce many pupils, he had many imitators, Lolli, Fiorillo, and above all, Paganini, whose talent was the most complete development of this model.

The Piedmontese school, founded by Somis, was destined to become the most fruitful in first-class talent. Besides Leclair, his nephew Schabran, or Chabran, became celebrated at Paris in 1751. Giardini, a model of grace, and above all Pugnani, who, endowed with a highly developed organisation, exercised a great influence upon the art, by the grandeur of his executive style, the variety of his bowing, and the improvements he introduced into the form of the concerto, as regards the effect of solos. Having become the leader of the Piedmontese school, Pugnani arrived at the zenith of his glory in maturing and forming the purer, beautiful, and brilliant talent of Viotti, who subsequently became both the model and despair of the violinists of every country.

Contemporary with Pugnani, Gaviniès effected for the French school at Paris what the Piedmontese violinist effected at Turin for the Italian school. Mechanism of the bow, which renders every difficulty easy, perfect intonation, imposing style, expression replete with charm and feeling; such were the qualities which excited Viotti when he heard Gaviniès, whom he called "le Tartini français." The talent of this artist was especially appreciated at its full value upon various occasions at concerts of sacred music, where other violinists of incontestable merit had performed. He bore away the palm after contesting it with Pugnani, Domenico Ferrari, and John Stamitz.

The arrival of Viotti in Paris produced a sensation difficult to describe. No performer had been heard who had attained so high a degree of perfection—no artist had possessed so fine a tone, such sustained elegance, such fire, and a style so varied. The fancy which was developed in his concertos increased the delight he produced in his auditory; his compositions for the Violin were as superior to those which had been previously heard as his execution surpassed that of all his predecessors and rivals. When this beautiful music became known, the rage for the concertos of Jarnowick became extinct, and the French school adopted more enlarged views. Viotti made few pupils; but there was one who alone was worth an entire school: Rode, who possessed all the brilliant qualifications of his master. There are few alive at the present day who have heard this artist in his prime, when he played at the concerts in the Rue Feydeau and at the Opera; but those artists who did will never forget the model of perfection which entranced them. It is an interesting remark, which I deem it a duty to make, that from Corelli to Rode there is no hiatus in the school—for Corelli was the master of Somis, Somis of Pugnani, Pugnani of Viotti, and Viotti of Rode.

When the talent of Rode was at its zenith, two other violinists rendered the French school illustrious. First, Rodolphe Kreutzer, the son of one of the Court musicians, who was born at Versailles in 1766, and was a pupil of Anthony Stamitz, a German violinist, who founded a school. Kreutzer at first adopted the narrow style of his master; but, under the guidance of Gaviniès, and after hearing Viotti, his method became broader, more brilliant, and bold beyond conception. His tone was full rather than mellow; and his manner of expression less remarkable than his mastery of difficulties. His great quality was originality, being no follower of any system, and obeying only the impulsion of his own energetic sensibility. Kreutzer founded a school, and made many pupils, who have taken advantage of his qualities, and who generally, are remarked for their brilliancy of execution.

Baillot, of whom I have still to speak, was not only a great violinist by the readiest and most varied mechanism imaginable, but he was a poet by his exquisite feeling for the beauties of music and his ready conception of the style necessary for imparting the true character of each composition. Pollani, pupil of Nardini, was one of Baillot's masters; but the immense natural talent of Baillot formed the rich basis of his own fancy; a great solo performer, he never went to the extent of his vast capabilities, if the work he was to interpret failed to awaken his appreciation. At the Opera, where he was engaged to play the solos for dancing, he was only the shadow of himself; but when at annual meetings for the performance of quartetts and quintetts, with the genius of Boccherini, of Haydn, of Mozart, and of

Beethoven, his enthusiasm was aroused; he became sublime and unequalled for his varied accentuation, the various shadings of expression, and the poetry of his ideas. His bow was magical; and every note under his fingers became an eloquent inspiration. Baillot was not only a great violinist—he was a great professor. The number of excellent violinists who were his pupils is considerable. His school produced Habeneck and Mazas—both of whom were eminent artists. Having become professor at the Conservatory of Paris, and the successor of his master, Habeneck produced some clever pupils, at the head of whom stands M. Alard, the present chief of the French school.

Lafont, too, one of the bright glories of the French school of violinists, was, at first, the pupil of Kreutzer. Dissatisfied with the style of his master, which did not sympathise with his own, he joined the school of Rode, which seemed formed for the development of his own qualities, combining grace, purity, elegance, and charm—qualities which, subsequently, with study, rendered him a perfect master of his art. The perfection of his intonation was so certain—the style of his bowing so seductive—his taste so exquisite in his ornament—that, if the sentiment of grandeur left anything to be desired, it was scarcely perceptible, it was lost in the rapture created by his grace and delicacy.

A new school has been formed. I allude to the Belgian school for the Violin, which numbers a nation of heroes, the chiefs of whom are De Bériot and Vieuxtemps; but, convinced that the history of one's friends is as difficult to write as that of one's enemies, I shall leave to future historians the agreeable task of handing down to posterity the names of these glories of their country.

Germany has produced several schools of violinists, whose principal qualities have been perfect intonation and neat execution; but which in the eighteenth century, especially, wanted a more powerful tone and broadness of execution. The prodigies invented by Walther in the seventeenth century, seem not to have left any traces. Italy and Bohemia were the cradles of two schools of German violinists, from whence the others proceeded.

Corelli, who disseminated everywhere the effects of his powerful influence, was first violinist in the chapel of the Margrave of Anspach, in 1699, when Pisendel, then choir-boy, became his pupil, and made such progress under his guidance, that he became first violinist of the chapel in 1702. This Pisendel, having become an eminent violinist, was attached to the Court of Saxony as master of the concerts, and opened, at Dresden, a school for the Violin. All the traditions of his master were transmitted to his pupils, but with the mannerism that was in vogue at the Court of Dresden. It was here the talent of Johann Gottlieb Graun, brother of the celebrated composer of that name, and master of the concerts of Frederick the Great, King of Prussia, was formed. Graun possessed sterling talent, of which he afforded many proofs, both by the pupils he made and by twenty-nine concertos for the Violin in manuscript, some of which I have seen, and which evince a remarkable degree of cleverness. In his youth, when he left the school of Pisendel, he went to Italy, and there received lessons from Tartini, whose style he adopted.

The school for the Violin founded in Bohemia, commenced by Konieseck of Prague. Konieseck is only known as having been the master of Francis Benda, a great artist, born at Althenatka, in Bohemia, the 23rd of November, 1709. His first master was a blind Jew, of the name of Lœbel, a very eminent violinist. He subsequently became the pupil of Konieseck, and acquired his brilliant style, though deficient in tone, which he transmitted to all his pupils. The school of Benda, from which proceeded his two sons, Ramnitz, Rust, Matthes, and several others, was celebrated for a long period in Germany. From this school came most of the Saxon and Prussian violinists. Benda, after the death of Graun, succeeded him as master of the concerts at the Court of Prussia in 1772, and died at Potsdam in 1786.

John Charles Stamitz, a remarkable violinist, and distinguished composer, emanated from Bohemia; he was born in 1719, his Violin master was a monk of the Abbey of Reichenau, the Father Czernohorsky. Being in the service of the Palatinate

Elector in 1745, Stamitz became the founder of the celebrated school of Mannheim, which produced the greater number of the German violinists of later days. The concertos of Stamitz, and a duet for one Violin, several times published, would alone suffice to prove the great capabilities of this artist: even did his pupils not bear evidence in favour of this judgment. Among his pupils were his two sons, Charles and Anthony, Canabich, Foerster, and several others. Christian Canabich succeeded his master; and his pupils were William Cramer, Danner, Ignace Fraenzel, all of whom were distinguished artists, but of different styles. Cramer and Danner possessed broadness in the style of bowing, but Fraenzel was a graceful and elegant performer, though his tone was somewhat thin. A pupil of Danner, John Frederick Eck, born at Mannheim in 1766, became a brilliant violinist of this school. This artist, director of the concerts of the Court of Munich, was the master of Spohr—at least, as far as talent can be formed, until individual organisation and meditation receive the stamp of personality. Louis Spohr has founded a Violin school in Germany, on a more extended and more vigorous scale than those of his predecessors. When Paganini heard him at Venice, he spoke of him in unqualified terms of approbation. This worthy artist has formed many pupils, who occupy most honourable positions in the large cities, and he has exposed the principles of his school in an extensive work, published by Haslinger, of Vienna, and subsequently translated into French and English.

Nicolo Paganini.

GENIUS—talent, whatever its extent—cannot always count upon popularity. Susceptibility of the highest conceptions of the most sublime creations, frequently fail in securing the attention of the multitude. How is this most coveted point to be attained? It would be difficult to arrive at any precise conclusion, from the fact that it applies to matters totally differing from each other; it is, however, perhaps possible to define the aggregation of qualities required to move the public in masses, by calling it "sympathetic wonderment." Fortunate boldness is its characteristic mark; originality its absolute condition. The most renowned popularities of the nineteenth century have each differed in their specialty,—Napoleon Bonaparte, Rossini, and Paganini. Many other names, doubtless, recall talents of the finest order, and personalities of the highest value; yet, notwithstanding their having been duly appreciated by the intelligent and enlightened classes, they have not called forth those outbursts of enthusiasm which have been manifested towards others during an entire generation. The truly popular name appears surrounded by its prestige, even to the lowest degrees of the social scale; such was the case with the prodigious artist who is the object of this notice.

Nicolo Paganini, the most extraordinary—the most renowned violinist of the nineteenth century—was born on February the 18th, 1784. His father, Antonio Paganini, a commercial broker, or simply a broker's clerk, according to some biographers, was passionately fond of music, and played upon the mandoline. His penetration soon discovered the aptitude of his son for this art. He resolved that study should develope it. His excessive severity would have probably led to results contrary to those he expected, had not the younger Paganini been endowed with the firm determination of becoming an artist. From the age of six years he was a musician, and played the Violin. The lessons he received from his father, as may be presumed, were not given in the most gentle manner. The ill-treatment to which he was subjected during this period of his youth, appears to have exercised a fatal influence upon his nervous and delicate constitution. From his first attempts he was imbued with the disposition to execute feats of strength and agility upon his instrument. His instinct urged him to attempt the most extraordinary things; his precocious skill exciting the astonishment of his young friends. His confidence in the future was not to be shaken, from the fact of his mother saying to him one day, "My son, you will be a great musician. An angel, radiant with beauty, appeared to me during the night, and, addressing me, spoke thus: 'If thou wouldst proffer a wish, it shall be accomplished.' I asked that you should become the greatest of all violinists, and the angel promised the fulfilment of my desire."

His father's lessons soon became useless, and Servetto, a musician of the theatre, at Genoa, became his teacher; but even he was not possessed of sufficient ability to be of benefit to this predestined artist. Paganini received his instructions for a short period only, and he was placed under Giacomo Costa, director of music, and principal violinist to the churches of Genoa, under whose care he progressed rapidly. He had now attained his eighth year, when he wrote his first sonata, which he unfortunately took no care of, and has been lost among many other of his productions. His countryman, Gnecco, a distinguished composer, encouraged the visits of the boy, and tendered counsel which doubtless aided him materially in his progress. Costa only gave him lessons for six months, during which period he obliged his pupil to play in the churches. But the master's instructions were not at all satisfactory to the pupil, who had already conceived a method of fingering and bowing.

Having reached his ninth year, the young *virtuoso* appeared in public, for the first time, in a concert at the large theatre of his native town, given by the excellent soprano Marchesi, with the vocalist Albertinatti. These two artists sang subsequently at a concert for Paganini's benefit, and in both these instances this extraordinary child played variations of his own composition on the French air, "la Carmagnole," amid the frenzied acclamations of an enthusiastic audience. About this period of his life the father was advised, by judicious friends, to place the boy under good masters of the Violin and composition; and he shortly after took him to Parma, where Alexandro Rolla then resided, so celebrated for his performance, as conductor of the orchestra, and as a composer. Paganini was now twelve years of age. The following anecdote, related by M. Schottky, and which Paganini published in a Vienna journal, furnishes interesting details of the master's first interview with the young artist:—"On arriving at Rolla's house, he said, we found him ill, and in bed. His wife conducted us into a room adjoining the one where the sick man lay, in order to concert with her husband, who, it appeared, was not at all dis posed to receive us. Perceiving upon the table of the chamber into which we were ushered a Violin, and the last concerto of Rolla, I took up the Violin and played the piece at first sight. Surprised at what he heard, the composer inquired the name of the *virtuoso* he had just heard. When he heard it was only a mere lad, he would not give credence to the fact unless by ocular demonstration. Thus satisfied, he told me, that he could teach me nothing, and recommended me to take lessons in composition from Paër." The evident desire evinced by Paganini to refute the supposition of his having received lessons from Rolla, is a singularity difficult to account for. Gervasoni, who knew him at Parma at this period, affirms* that he was the pupil of Rolla for several months. However, it was not Paër, then in Germany, who taught Paganini harmony and counterpoint, but Ghiretti, who

* "Nuova Teoria di Musica," &c. Parma, 1812. 1 vol., in 8vo (page 214). Gervasoni adds that no teacher could have conducted such an artist to the sublime height Paganini attained, and that nature alone could have directed him.

had directed the studies of Paër himself. During six months this precocious artist received three lessons weekly, and specially applied himself to the study of instrumentation. Even now Paganini was occupied in discovering new effects on his instrument. Frequent discussions took place between him and Rolla on the innovations which the young artist contemplated, and which he could, at this period, only execute imperfectly, whilst the severe taste of his master deprecated these bold attempts, except for the sake of occasional effects. It was, however, only after his return to Genoa, that Paganini wrote his first compositions for the Violin. This music was so difficult that he was obliged to study it himself with increasing perseverance, and to make constant efforts to solve problems unknown to all other violinists. He was seen to have tried the same passage in a thousand different ways during ten or twelve hours, and to be completely overwhelmed with fatigue at the end of the day. It is by this unexampled perseverance that he overcame difficulties which were considered insurmountable by contemporary artists, when he published a specimen in the shape of a collection of studies.

Quitting Parma, at the commencement of 1797, Paganini made his first professional tour with his father through all the principal towns in Lombardy, and commenced a reputation which increased daily from that period. On his return to Genoa, and after having, in solitude, made the efforts necessary for the development of his talent, he began to feel the weight of the chain by which he was held by his father, and determined to release himself from the ill-treatment to which he was still subjected under the paternal roof. His artistic soul revolted at this degrading slavery, and felt that some respect was due to him. A favourable opportunity alone was required to execute his design. This soon presented itself. The fête of St. Martin was celebrated annually at Lucca by a musical festival, to which persons flocked from every part of Italy. As this period approached, Paganini entreated his father to permit him to attend it, accompanied by his elder brother. His demand was at first met with a peremptory refusal; but the solicitations of the son, and the prayers of the mother, finally prevailed, and the heart of the young artist, at liberty for the first time, bounded with joy, and he set out agitated by dreams of success and happiness. At Lucca he was received with enthusiasm. Encouraged by this propitious débût, he visited Pisa, and some other towns, in all of which his success was unequivocal. The year 1799 had just commenced, and Paganini had not attained his fifteenth year. This is not the age of prudence. His moral education had been grossly neglected, and the severity which assailed his more youthful years, was not calculated to awaken him to the dangers of a life of freedom. Freed from restraint, and relishing the delights of his new-born independence, he formed connections with other artists, whose sole abilities seemed to consist in encouraging a taste for gambling in young men of family and means, and turning the tables upon them to their own advantage. Paganini, in this manner, frequently lost the produce of several concerts in one night, and was consequently often in a state of great embarrassment. His talent soon procured fresh resources, and time passed gaily enough, alternately between good and bad fortune. He was frequently reduced, by distress, to part with his Violin. In this condition he found himself at Leghorn, and was indebted to the kindness of a French merchant, (M. Livron), a distinguished amateur, for the loan of a Violin, an excellent Guarnieri. When the concert had concluded, Paganini brought it back to its owner, when this gentleman exclaimed, "Never will I profane strings which your fingers have touched; that instrument is now yours." This is the Violin Paganini afterwards used in all his concerts. A similar event occurred to him at Parma, but under different circumstances. Pasini, an eminent painter, and an excellent amateur performer on the Violin, had disbelieved the prodigious faculty imputed to Paganini, of playing the most difficult music at first sight, as well as if he had maturely studied it. He brought him a manuscript concerto, containing the most difficult passages, imagined almost by every performer as insurmountable, and placing in his hands an excellent instrument of Stradiuari, added, "This instrument shall be yours, if you can play, in a masterly manner, that concerto at first sight." "If that is the case," replied Paganini, "you may bid adieu to it," and he forthwith, by his exquisite performance of the piece, threw Pasini into extatic admiration.

Adventures of every kind characterise this period of Paganini's early days; the enthusiasm of art, love, and gambling, divided his time, despite the warnings of a delicate constitution, which proclaimed the necessity of great care. Heedless of everything, he continued his career of dissipation, until the prostration of all his faculties forced a respite. He would then lie up for several weeks, in a state of absolute repose, until, with refreshed energies, he recommenced his artistic career and wandering life. Unexpected resources occasionally relieved him from positive poverty. In this position, at seventeen years of age, being at Leghorn, in 1801, he became acquainted with a wealthy Swedish amateur, whose favourite instrument was the bassoon. Complaining that he could meet with no music for his instrument, sufficiently difficult for his talent, Paganini provided him with compositions almost impracticable, for which he was richly rewarded. It was to be feared that this dissolute life would ultimately deprive the world of his marvellous talent, when an unforeseen and important circumstance, related by himself, ended his fatal passion for gambling.

"I shall never forget," he said, "that I one day, placed myself in a position which was to decide my future. The Prince of —— had, for some time, coveted the possession of my Violin—the only one I possessed at that period, and which I still have. He, on one particular occasion, was extremely anxious that I should mention the sum for which I would dispose of it; but, not wishing to part with my instrument, I declared I would not sell it for 250 gold napoleons. Some time after the Prince said to me that I was, doubtless, only speaking in jest in asking such a sum, but that he would be willing to give me 2,000 francs. I was, at this moment, in the greatest want of money to meet a debt of honour I had incurred at play, and was almost tempted to accept the proffered amount, when I received an invitation to a party that evening at a friend's house. All my capital consisted of thirty francs, as I had disposed of all my jewels, watch, rings, and brooches, &c. I resolved on risking this last resource; and, if fortune proved fickle, to sell my Violin to the Prince and to proceed to St. Petersburg, without instrument or luggage, with the view of re-establishing my affairs; my thirty francs were reduced to three, and I fancied myself on the road to Russia, when suddenly my fortune took a sudden turn; and, with the small remains of my capital I won 160 francs. This amount saved my Violin, and completely set me up. From that day I abjured gambling—to which I had sacrificed part of my youth—convinced that a gamester is an object of contempt to all well-regulated minds."

Although he was still in the prime of youth, Paganini knew of nothing but success and profit, when, during one of those hallucinations to which all great artists are subject, the Violin lost its attractions in his eyes. A lady of rank having fallen desperately in love with him, and the feeling being reciprocated, he withdrew with her to an estate she possessed in Tuscany.* This lady played the Guitar, and Paganini imbibed a taste for that instrument, and applied himself as sedulously to its practice as he had formerly done with the Violin. He soon discovered new resources, which he imparted to his friend; and during a period of three years, he devoted all the energies of his mind to its study, and to agricultural pursuits, for which the lady's estate afforded him ample opportunities. It was at this period he wrote his two sonatas for Guitar and Violin, which form his second and third works.

Love cools with time in a castle as in a cottage. Paganini discovered this; all his former penchant for the Violin returned, and he decided on resuming his travels. On his return to Genoa, in 1804, he occupied himself solely with composition, and wrote here his fourth work which consists of four grand

* This circumstance in the life of Paganini made very little impression upon me when he related it to me, as I was only interested in his artistic career: later, this anecdote appeared important to establish the chronological order of his life, as will be hereafter seen.

quartetts for Violin, Viol, Guitar, and Violoncello; and bravura variations for Violin, on an original theme, with Guitar accompaniment, which forms his fifth work. It appears too, that at this period he gave instruction on the Violin to Catarina Calcagno,* born at Genoa, in 1797, who, at the age of fifteen, astounded Italy by the boldness of her style. All traces of her seem lost after 1816. Towards the middle of 1805, Paganini left Genoa, to undertake a new tour in Italy. The first town he visited was Lucca, the scene of his first successes. Here he again created so great a sensation by a concerto he performed at a nocturnal festival in a convent chapel, that the monks were obliged to leave their stalls, in order to repress the applause which burst forth despite the sanctity of the place. He was then twenty-one years of age. The principality of Lucca and Piombino had been organised in the month of March, of the same year, in favour of the Princess Eliza, sister of Napoleon, and the wife of Prince Bacciochi. The Court had fixed its residence in the town of Lucca. The great reputation of the violinist induced the Princess to offer him the posts of director of her private music, and conductor of the opera orchestra. Notwithstanding his propensity for independence of action, and although the emoluments were scanty, the position pleased him, and he accepted it. The Prince Bacciochi received instruction from him on the Violin. The Princess, who had appreciated the originality of his talent, induced him to extend his discoveries of novel effects upon the instrument. To convince him of the interest he had inspired her with, she granted him the grade of captain in the royal gendarmerie, so that he might be admitted with his brilliant costume to all the great Court receptions. Paganini added many novelties to those which characterised his talent. Thus, seeking to vary the effect of his instrument at the Court concerts, where it was his duty to play, he removed the second and third strings, and composed a dialogue for the first and fourth strings. He has related this circumstance himself nearly in these terms:—

* Gervasoni, "Nuova Teoria di Musica," page 103.

"At Lucca I directed the orchestra when the reigning family honoured the opera with their presence. I was often called upon to play at Court: and then, I organised fortnightly concerts. The Princess Eliza always withdrew before the termination, as my harmonic sounds irritated her nerves. A lady, whom I had long loved without having avowed my passion, attended the concerts with great regularity. I fancied I perceived that I was the object of her assiduous visits. Insensibly our mutual passion increased; but important motives rendered prudence and mystery necessary; our love in consequence became more violent. I had promised her, on one occasion, that, at the following concert, I would introduce a musical piece which should bear allusion to our relative positions; and I announced to the Court a novelty under the title of "Scène amoureuse." Curiosity rose to the highest pitch; but the surprise of all present at Court was extreme, when I entered the saloon with a Violin with only two strings. I had only retained the first and the fourth. The former was to express the sentiments of a young girl, the other was to express the passionate language of a lover. I had composed a kind of dialogue, in which the most tender accents followed the outbursts of jealousy. At one time, chords representing most tender appeals, at another, plaintive reproaches; cries of joy and anger, felicity and pain. Then followed the reconciliation; and the lovers, more persuaded than ever, executed a *pas de deux*, which terminated in a brilliant coda. This novelty was eminently successful. I do not speak of the languishing looks which the goddess of my thoughts darted at me. The Princess Eliza lauded me to the skies; and said to me in the most gracious manner possible, 'You have just performed impossibilities; would not a single string suffice for your talent?' I promised to make the attempt. The idea delighted me; and, some weeks after, I composed my military sonata, entitled "Napoleon," which I performed on the 25th of August, before a numerous and brilliant Court. Its success far surpassed my expectations. My predilection for the G string dates from this period. All I wrote for this string was received with enthusiasm, and I daily acquired greater facility upon it: hence I obtained the mastery of it, which you know, and should no longer surprise you."

In the summer of 1808, Paganini obtained leave to travel, and quitted Lucca, never more to return. As the sister of Napoleon had become Grand Duchess of Tuscany, she fixed her residence at Florence, with all her Court, where the great artist retained his position.* He went to Leghorn, where, seven years previously, he had met with so much success. Here he was not received with the warmth extended to him on his former visit; but his talent soon overcame the coldness evinced towards him. He has related, with much humour, a series of tribulations which happened to him upon the occasion of his first concert there. "A nail," he said, "had run into my heel, and I came on limping, at which the audience laughed. At the moment I was about to commence my concerto, the candles of my desk fell out. (Another laugh.) At the end of the first few bars of the solo, my first string broke, which increased the hilarity of the audience, but I played the piece on the three strings—and the grins quickly changed into acclamations of applause." The broken string frequently occurred afterwards; and Paganini has been accused of using it as a means of success, having previously practised upon the three strings, pieces which appear to require the use of the first also.

From Leghorn he went to Turin, where the Princess Pauline Borghese, sister of Napoleon, the Prince, her husband, and suite, were sojourning. Blangini, then attached to the service of the Princess as director of music (1808 or 1809), there heard the illustrious violinist at several concerts; and spoke of him to me, on his return to Paris, with unbounded admiration. It was at Turin that Paganini was first attacked with internal inflammation, which subsequently so debilitated his health, as frequently to cause long interruptions to his travels, and his series of concerts. He was nearly convalescent, when he was recalled to the Court of Florence, in the month of October, 1809, for the concerts which were to be given on the occasion of peace between France and

* Gervasoni, "Nuova Teoria di Musica," page 214.

Austria. It was at this period that my friend, the celebrated sculptor, Bartolini, executed a bust of Paganini, which I saw in his studio at Florence, in 1841. An excellent work by M. Conestabile, which has just appeared, and which only reached me a few days ago,* furnishes me with information as to the manner Paganini was employed in 1810. It will be found (p. 58) that he must have left Florence about December, 1809, to visit Romagna and Lombardy; that he gave concerts at the old theatre of Cesena; that he afterwards produced an extraordinary sensation at a concert given at Rimini, the 22nd of January, 1810. This information was extracted by M. Conestabile, from manuscript memoirs by M. Giangi, an amateur composer, relating to the town of Rimini. It is probable he afterwards visited the other cities of Central Italy, Ravenna, Forli, Imola, and Faenza; but this is not certain. It appears also about the same period he met with an adventure at Ferrara that nearly cost him his life. He had gone to Bologna with a friend, and purposed giving some concerts there. Arrangements were already made with the manager, and rehearsals appointed, when, at the moment the rehearsal was about to commence, Marcolini, who was to sing at the concert, capriciously refused to do so. Disconcerted by this *contretemps*, Paganini sought the aid of Madame Pallerini, the principal dancer of the theatre, but who possessed a most agreeable voice, which she only cultivated for herself and her friends. Vanquished by the solicitations of the great violinist, she consented to sing at the concert; but when she presented herself to the public, fear overpowered her—she sang with timidity—and when she retired, encouraged by the kind applause which rewarded her efforts, a piercing hiss was heard. Maddened with rage, Paganini vowed to avenge this outrage at the end of the concert. As he was about to commence his last solo, he announced to the public that he purposed imitating the notes and cries of various animals. After having imitated the chirping of certain birds, cock-crowing,

* "Vita di Paganini di Genova, scritta ed illustrata da Giancarlo Conestabile. Perugia, Tipografia di Vincenzo Bartilli, 1851." 1 vol., in 8vo, 317 pages.

the mewing of a cat, and the barking of a dog, he advanced to the footlights, and while imitating the braying of an ass, he called out "This for the men who hissed" (Questo è per quelli che han fischiato!) He was convinced this repartee would excite laughter, and the hissers be hooted; but the pit rose to a man, vociferating, and rushing forward to the orchestra, which they literally scaled. Paganini had only time to escape, by hasty flight, the dangers that menaced him. It was only after he was safely at home, that he learned the cause of this fearful tumult. He was told that the peasantry in the suburbs of Ferrara entertain peculiar ill feelings towards the residents of that town—considering them as a community of idiots, and compare them to asses. Hence, any resident of the suburb, if questioned from whence he came, never admits it is from Ferrara, but vociferates a vigorous hee-haw. The audience present at Paganini's concert considered this a personal allusion to themselves; the result was, that the authorities withdrew their permission and prohibited the continuation of his concerts. Since then, Paganini was never heard again at Ferrara.

Gervasoni relates* that on the 16th of August, 1811, Paganini gave a concert at Parma, at which he produced an immense sensation, both upon artists and amateurs, particularly in his variations on the fourth string. It would appear that from Parma he returned to his duties at the Court of Florence. Here he probably remained during the year 1812, for no information of him in other places, during this period, is met with. He was, there can be little doubt, obliged to return occasionally to the capital of Tuscany to fulfil his duties. Here, about the end of 1812, or the commencement of 1813, occurred the adventure which obliged him suddenly to quit the service of the Grand Duchess, and leave the town. This adventure had been certified to M. Conestabile by ocular witnesses, in nearly the following terms:—At a grand Court gala, where a concert preceded a ball, Paganini, who directed the former, and was to have performed, appeared in the orchestra in his uniform of captain of the royal gendarmerie. The Princess, as soon as she perceived this, sent

* Loc. cit.

her commands that the uniform was to be replaced by evening dress. He replied that his commission allowed him to wear the uniform, and refused to change it. The command was repeated during the concert and again met with refusal; and to prove that he defied the orders of the Grand Duchess, he appeared at the ball in his uniform. Moreover, in order to show that he did not care what might be thought of the insult proffered to him, he walked up and down the room after the ball had commenced. Nevertheless, convinced that although reason and right were both in his favour, absolutism prevailed at Court, and his defiance might endanger his liberty, he quitted Florence during the night, and directed his steps towards Lombardy. The most tempting offers, and the promise of the Grand Duchess's leniency, proved unavailing to induce him to return.* Delighted at finding himself his own master, he determined never again to accept a fixed position, however tempting the offer.

Being at Milan in the spring of 1813, he witnessed, at the Theatre La Scala, the ballet of "Il Noce di Benevento" by Virgano, the music of which was by Süssmayer.† It was from this ballet that Paganini took the theme of his celebrated variations "le Streghe," (the Witches), from the air being that to which the witches appeared. While busied with these variations, and making arrangements for his concerts, he was again seized with a return of his former malady, and several months elapsed before he could appear in public. It was only on the 29th of October following he was enabled to give his first concert, when he excited a sensation which the journals of Italy and Germany made known to the whole world.

Paganini always evinced an extraordinary predilection for Milan, to which city he was much attached. Not only did he

* From the sentiments which induced the Grand Duchess to overlook his insubordination, and from certain innuendoes which have escaped the pen of M. Conestabile, inferences may be drawn, which delicacy dictates should not be mentioned unreservedly.

† An artist of great merit, author of several operas, and who continued the Requiem of Mozart.

reside there the greater part of 1813, with the exception of his visit to Genoa, but also, until the month of September, 1814, visiting it three times during five years, residing there for a long period, and giving thirty-seven concerts. In 1813 he gave eleven, some at La Scala, and others at the Theatre Carcano; and, after a repose of some months, another series at the Theatre Rè, in 1814. In the month of October of that year he went to Bologna, where he saw Rossini for the first time, and commenced a friendship which became strengthened at Rome, in 1817, and at Paris in 1831. Rossini produced his "Aureliano in Palmira," in December, 1813, at Milan, at which period Paganini was at Genoa, so that these artists had never yet met each other until Rossini was about leaving Bologna, to write his "Turco in Italia," at Milan.

Up to the year 1828, Paganini had made three times the round of Italy. In 1815 he returned to Romagna, and having given some concerts there, stopped at Ancona. Here his malady returned to him for several months, and he then proceeded to Genoa, about the commencement of 1816, while Lafont was giving concerts at Milan. Anxious to hear the French violinist, he repaired thither, where a rivalry ensued, which was much spoken of, and appreciated in various ways, according to the bias of school and nationality. Lafont, who frequently related to me the circumstances of this meeting, was perfectly convinced that he was the victor. It is interesting to hear Paganini's relation of this circumstance of his life:—"Being at Genoa, in March, 1816, I heard that Lafont was giving concerts at Milan, for which city I immediately started, for the purpose of hearing him. His performance pleased me exceedingly. A week afterwards I gave a concert at the Theatre La Scala, to make myself known to him. The next day Lafont proposed we should both perform on the same evening. I excused myself by saying that such experiments were always impolitic, as the public invariably looked upon such matters as duels, in which there was always a victim, and that it would be so in this case; for as he was acknowledged the best violinist in France, so the public indulgently considered me as the best of Italian violinists. Lafont not looking at it in this light, I was obliged to accept the challenge. I allowed him to regulate the programme, which he did in the following manner :—We each in turn played one of our own compositions, after which we played together the "Symphonie concertante" of Kreutzer, for two Violins. In this I did not deviate in the least from the author's text, while we both were playing our own parts; but in the solos I yielded to my own imagination, and introduced several novelties, which seemed to annoy my adversary. Then followed a Russian air, with variations, by Lafont, and I finished the concert with my variations on "le Streghe." Lafont probably surpassed me in tone, but the applause which followed my efforts convinced me I did not suffer by comparison." Lafont, it cannot be denied, acted imprudently under the circumstances, for although it may be admitted he possessed more purely classical qualities, and was more in accordance with French taste than Paganini, although his tone was fuller, and more equal, yet, in original fancy, poetry of execution, and mastery of difficulties, he could not place himself in juxtaposition with his antagonist. In a concert, at the Conservatory of Paris, in 1816, the palm would have been awarded to him, but, with an Italian public, athirst for novelty and originality, his failure was certain.

A similar circumstance occurred two years later, when Paganini had returned to Placentia to give concerts. The Polish violinist, Lipinski,* was then there (1818). He had sought Paganini without success at Venice, Verona, and Milan, and had abandoned all hopes of meeting him, when a concert bill was put into his hands, which announced that they were then together in the same town. Paganini gave six concerts in this town; and, at the sixth, played a concerted symphony with Lipinski, which was much applauded. They frequently met at each other's residence and improvised together. Some time after, Lipinski dedicated to him one of his works † as a tribute of respect; but when they again

* Who subsequently became principal Violin soloist at the Chapel of the King of Saxony.

† Tre Capricci per il Violino, dedicati al esimio professore Nicolo Paganini, da Carlo Lipinski. Leipzig: Breitkopf und Härtel, 1827.

PAGANINI'S VIOLIN,

IN THE MUNICIPAL PALACE AT GENOA.

From "The Violin: its Famous Makers and their Imitators." (By kind permission of Mr. G. Hart.)

met at Warsaw, in 1829, a journal, speaking of a concert which the Polish violinist had just given, and lauding his talent, took occasion to depreciate the ability of Paganini, and to accuse the virtuoso of charlatanism. Other journals defended the Genoese violinist, and undervalued the merit of Lipinski, who deemed it a duty publicly to exculpate himself from the suspicion of having been connected with the discourteous attack directed towards his illustrious competitor. Paganini did not seem at all concerned about the matter, but the intimacy of the two artists ceased.

From Milan, Paganini repaired to Venice, in the summer of 1816, where he remained for upwards of a year, to restore his health, which had for some time been in a declining state; he also gave some concerts. This protracted sojourn at Venice is mentioned in the "Leipziger Musikalische Zeitung," of July the 23rd, 1817, by a correspondent, who thus alludes to the subject:—

"The celebrated violinist, Paganini, has at last quitted Venice, where he has been sojourning for more than twelve months, and has returned to Genoa, his native town, taking Milan in his route."

In the same year (1817) he arrived at Rome, and found Rossini there busy in producing his "Cenerentola." Several concerts which he gave there during the Carnival excited the greatest enthusiasm. He also frequently played at the palace of the Count de Kaunitz, ambassador of Austria, where he met Count Metternich, who urgently pressed him to visit Vienna. From this time Paganini formed the project of leaving Italy to visit the principal cities of Germany and France; however, the uncertain state of his health, which, at times, placed his life in danger, prevented him from realising his project at this period. Besides, he had not yet visited Naples and Sicily—and he had long entertained a strong desire of doing so; however, it does not seem that he visited, at this time, that portion of the Peninsula, for we hear of him in Upper Italy, giving concerts at Verona, at Placentia, at Turin, at Florence, and throughout Tuscany, during 1818, and a portion of 1819.* It was only in the latter year that he arrived at Naples. It is a very remarkable circumstance that he appeared there in a manner unworthy of his great name; for, instead of giving his first concerts at the San Carlo, he modestly commenced at the theatre Il Fondo. It is true that, at the period he arrived—namely in the middle of the summer, the theatrical performances are more frequently given at the Fondo than at San Carlo.

On his arrival at Naples, Paganini found several artists indisposed towards him. They doubted the reality of the prodigies attributed to him, and awaited a failure. To put his talent to the test, the young composer, Danna, recently from the Conservatory, was engaged to write a quartett, containing every species of difficulty, convinced that the great violinist would not vanquish them. He was, therefore, invited to a musical re-union, where he met the violinist Onorio de Vito, the composer Danna, the violinist and director of music Festa, and the violoncellist Ciandelli. The piece was immediately given to him to play at first sight. Understanding the snare that was laid for him, he merely glanced at it, and played it as if he had been familiar with it. Amazed and confounded at what they had heard, the highest approbation was awarded to him, and he was proclaimed a miracle.

It was during this sojourn at Naples, that Paganini met with one of the most singular adventures of his extraordinary life. An alarming relapse of his malady took place; and, thinking that any current of air was injurious to him, he took an apartment in a part of the town called Petrajo, below Sant Elmo; but meeting here that

* M. Conestabile places Paganini's first visit to Naples and Sicily immediately after the concerts at Rome during the Carnival, but I have found no traces of his having done so in the musical journals, the Italian newspapers, and the almanacks, of that period (1818). It would be difficult to understand that, in a short time, Paganini could have given several concerts at the Theatre Fondo, others at San Carlo, at Naples, then at Palermo; and that he should have left Upper Italy, Piedmont, and Tuscany, to return to Naples and Sicily in 1819. I believe his first visit to Naples only took place in 1819. In the months of December, 1818, and January, 1819, he gave four concerts at the Theatre Carignano of Turin; in the February following he gave concerts at Florence, and in June and July some at Naples.

which he most sought to avoid, and his health daily becoming worse, it was reported that he was consumptive. At Naples, the opinion prevailed that consumption is contagious. His landlord, alarmed at having in his house one who was supposed to be dying of this malady, had the inhumanity to turn him out into the street, with all he possessed. Fortunately, the violoncellist Ciandelli, the friend of Paganini, happened to be passing, and, incensed at this act of cruelty, which might have proved fatal to the great artist, belaboured the barbarian unmercifully with a stick he carried, and then had his friend conveyed to a comfortable lodging, where every attention was paid to him. Paganini recovered sufficiently to give concerts.

Having returned to Milan, in March, 1820, Paganini took part in founding a society of musical amateurs, which adopted the name of "Gli Orfei," for the performance of the classical works of the old masters. He conducted several of this society's concerts who, in testimony of gratitude and admiration, presented him with medals and crowns. Paganini's predilection for the capital of Lombardy detained him there until December. He then went to Rome, and arrived while Rossini was producing his "Matilda di Sabran," at the Apollo Theatre. On the day of the general rehearsal, the leader of the orchestra was seized with apoplexy. This unexpected event was a source of great embarrassment to the composer, inasmuch as the talent of the musicians was below mediocrity. As soon as this circumstance reached Paganini, he flew to his friend's assistance, attended the general rehearsal, and led the three first representations with an energy that struck the band with amazement.

In May, 1821, Paganini left Rome to return to Naples. Kandler met him here during the summer. He gave concerts at the Fondo, and at the Teatro Nuovo. This literary musician has given an account in the "Morgenblatt" (1821, No. 290) of the extraordinary impression this "Hercules of Violinists," as he called him, made upon him. The account is filled with expressions of unbounded admiration.

From Naples Paganini went to Palermo, and gave concerts,

which were but poorly attended, attributed by the correspondent of the "Leipziger Musikalische Zeitung" to the indifference of the Sicilians for instrumental music. His stay here was of short duration, for we find him at Venice, then at Placentia, at the commencement of 1822. In April of the same year he gave concerts at Milan, his return being hailed with the warmest tokens of delight, and with a success surpassing all his former visits. He was now seriously preoccupied with his visit to Germany, as projected by Count Metternich; but during an excursion to Pavia, he again fell seriously ill, in January, 1823, and his life was despaired of. He had scarcely recovered when he proceeded to Turin, where a similar welcome and success awaited him. His health was, however, extremely delicate, and the necessity of repose so manifest, that he was obliged to return to his native air. Some months of inaction and calm, passed at Genoa, renewed his health and strength sufficiently to enable him to give concerts at the Theatre Saint Augustin, to which his fellow-townsfolk flocked in crowds. These concerts took place in the month of May, 1824, after which he repaired to Milan. Here he played at La Scala, on the 12th of June of the same year, and was received with acclamations which denoted the intense interest his health had excited. Some days after, he returned to Genoa, and gave two concerts, the first on the 30th of June, the second on the 7th of July following.

Paganini seemed to have recovered all his pristine health and strength, for in the month of November in the same year his talent seemed to be greater than ever at the concerts he gave at Venice. The title of "Filarmonico," which then followed his name on his concert bills, gave rise to polemical discussions. Enemies, which great talent invariably creates, pretended that the Genoese violinist sought to induce the belief that he was a member of the Academy of Philharmonics of Bologna; although such was not the case, his admirers replied that the Academy would be honoured if Paganini condescended to become one. He terminated the discussion by declaring that his assuming the addition to his name was merely a declaration of his love for the art.

In January, 1825, Paganini gave two concerts at Trieste; thence he proceeded to Naples, for the third time, and met with a renewal of his former triumphs. In the summer he returned to Palermo, and this time his success was unparalleled. The delicious climate of Sicily was so agreeable to him that he remained here a year, giving here and there occasional concerts, but enjoying long intervals of repose. This lengthened sojourn in such a favourable climate restored him to better health than he had experienced for a long period, and he returned to his project of quitting Italy. However, before doing so, he wished to return to several towns of which he retained so many delightful reminiscences, and went to Trieste in the summer of 1826, then to Venice, and finally to Rome, where he gave five concerts at the Theatre Argentina, each of which was a separate ovation. On the 5th of April, 1827, Pope Leo the Twelfth decorated him with the Order of the Golden Spur, in token of his admiration of his great talent. From Rome he went to Florence, where he was detained by a disease in one of his legs, which remained uncured for a very long period. He went to Milan, where he was warmly received by his friends, and on the 2nd of March, 1828, he quitted this town and proceeded to Vienna, where he arrived the 16th of the same month.

On the 29th of March, the first concert of this great artist threw the Viennese population into an indescribable paroxysm of enthusiasm. "The first note he played on his Guarnerius (says M. Schilling, in poetical style, in his "Universal-Lexicon der Musik") —indeed, from his first step into the room—his reputation was decided in Germany. Acted upon as by an electric spark, a brilliant halo of glory appeared to invest his whole person; he stood before us like a miraculous apparition in the domain of art." The Vienna journals were unlimited in hyperbolical expressions of admiration; and the immense crowd whom he had enchanted at this concert, unceasingly poured forth hymns of praise to the glory of the enchanter, for two months. The most eminent artists of the Austrian capital, Mayseder, Jansa, Slawich, Léon de St. Lubin, Strebinger, Böhm, and others, all admitted his performance to be incomparable. Other concerts given on the 13th, 16th, 18th, of April, etc., created universal intoxication. Verses appeared in every publication—medals were struck—the name of Paganini engrossing all; and, as M. Schottky remarks, everything was à la Paganini. Fashion assumed his name. Hats, dresses, gloves, shoes, etc., bore his name. Cooks designated certain productions after him; and any extraordinary stroke at billiards was compared to a bow movement of the artist. His portrait appeared on snuff-boxes and cigar-cases; in fact, his bust surmounted the walking-sticks of fashionable men. After a concert given for the benefit of the poor, the magistrate of Vienna presented to Paganini the large gold medal of St. Salvator, and the Emperor conferred upon him the title of virtuoso of his private band.

A lengthened sojourn in the capital of Austria, and numerous concerts, did not in the least diminish the impression Paganini had created on his arrival. The same ovations were showered upon him in every town of Germany. Prague, from certain traditionary opposition to the musical opinions of Vienna, alone received him coldly; but Berlin so amply avenged this indifference, that he exclaimed at his first concert, "Here is my Vienna public!" After an uninterrupted series of triumphs, during three years, in Austria, Bohemia, Saxony, Poland, Bavaria, Prussia, and in the Rhenish provinces, after unceasing ovations of Vienna, Dresden, Berlin, and Frankfort, the celebrated artist arrived at Paris, and gave his first concert at the Opera, the 9th of March, 1831. His studies for the Violin, which had been published there for some time—a species of enigma which had perplexed every violinist; the European fame of the artist, his travels and triumphs, raised the curiosity of the artists and the public. It is impossible to describe the enthusiasm his first concert created—it was universal frenzy. Tumultuous applause preceded and followed all his performances, the audience rose *en masse* to recall him after each, and nothing was heard but general approbation and amazement. The same enthusiasm prevailed during his entire stay in Paris.

Towards the middle of May he left this city, and proceeded to

London, where he was expected with the utmost impatience, but not with that artistic and perceptive interest with which he had been received at Paris. The high prices of admission charged for his concerts drew down the reprobation of the English journals, as if the artist was not privileged to put what price he pleased upon his talent, or that they were perforce obliged to go and hear him. The concerts at London, at which Paganini performed, and his professional tour through England, Scotland, and Ireland, produced an immense amount of money; this was a large fortune, to which he added considerably afterwards, during his visits to France and Belgium. He has been reproached with having sold himself to an English speculator for a certain time and a definite sum: a system which many artists have since adopted, though it is repugnant both to art and the dignity of the artist. Yet the great care necessary for the organisation of concerts, the difficulties encountered by an artist in England, certainly offer some apology for its adoption. The scandalous manner in which the managements plunder the artists—the toll claimed by the band, charitable institutions, printers, advertisements, lighting, servants, &c., &c., &c., offer so many interruptions to the calm serenity necessary for the display of talent, that the artist can scarcely be blamed for ridding himself of these annoyances by concluding a compact by which he is assured a specific sum.*

After an absence of six years, Paganini again set foot on his native soil. The wealth he had amassed in his European tour, placed him in a position of great independence. He sought to place this to advantage, yet was undecided what part of the Peninsula he would select as his place of abode. His former predilection was for Tuscany; but, among the various properties he purchased, was a charming country house in the environs of

* M. Fétis ought by this time to be aware that an artist suffers from any of these difficulties in a less degree in England than in any country of Europe; in no part of the world is the true merit or just talent of a musician sooner discerned, or more justly rewarded, than in England; yet, at the same time, it must be conceded that charlatanism, both native and foreign, has long been rampant and held a sway, as far as music is concerned, in this country, quite revolting to a true artist.—*Translator's Note.*

Parma, called la Villa Gajona—here he decided on residing. Various projects occupied him at this period, the most important of which was the publication of his compositions—a publication which was ardently desired by all violinists, under the impression that they would arrive at the secret of his marvellous talent. During his stay in London, M. Troupenas, one of the most eminent publishers in Paris at that time, arrived there for the purpose of purchasing the copyright of his manuscripts; yet, although M. Troupenas was accustomed to pay large sums to celebrated authors, whose works he published, particularly Rossini and Auber, he could not come to terms with the great violinist. M. Troupenas has frequently told me that the sum asked by Paganini for his manuscripts was so considerable, that a continuous sale during ten years would not have reimbursed him. Afterwards, at Brussels, Paganini told me he contemplated publishing his works himself; but, not having yet abandoned giving concerts, he conceived the singular idea of arranging his music for the Pianoforte.

On returning to Italy, where he was almost worshipped by his countrymen, from the great triumphs he had obtained, and the honours conferred on him by foreign potentates, he was received with the most marked degree of respect. On the 14th of November, 1834, he gave a concert at Placentia, for the benefit of the poor. The following 12th of December, he played at the Court of Maria Louisa, Duchess of Parma, from whom he received the imperial Order of St. George. During the year 1835, Paganini alternately resided at Genoa, Milan, and at his retreat near Parma. The cholera, which was then raging at Genoa, gave rise to the rumour that he had fallen a victim to the infection. This event was announced in the public papers, in which there apppeared necrological notices; but, although his health was lamentably bad, he escaped the cholera.

In 1836, some speculators induced him to lend the aid of his name and talent to establish a casino, of which music was the pretext, but gambling the real object. This establishment, which was situated in the most fashionable locality of Paris, was opened with considerable splendour at the end of November, 1837, under the name of Casino Paganini; but the Government refused to authorize its opening as a gambling house, and the speculators were reduced to give concerts, the proceeds of which were far exceeded by the expenses of the undertaking. Under the necessity of meeting the engagement entered into for this purpose, the great artist withdrew from his country house near Parma, and proceeded by way of Piedmont. At Turin, together with the guitarist Legnani, he gave a concert on the 9th of June, for the benefit of the poor; and he then proceeded by way of Lyons, notwithstanding his ill state of health, and arrived at Paris oppressed with fatigue and suffering. The decline of his health was manifest; and his wasted strength precluded the possibility of his playing at the Casino. As the price of his painful journey to Paris, and the loss of his health, a law suit was commenced against him, which he lost; the judges, without having heard his defence, condemned him to pay 50,000f. to the creditors of the speculation, and he was to be deprived of his liberty until that amount was paid.

When this decision was pronounced, Paganini was dying—his malady, which was phthisis of the larynx, had increased since the commencement of 1839. The medical men advised him to proceed to Marseilles, the climate of which they considered favourable to his health. He followed their advice, and travelled by slow stages to the south. His great energy struggled against the illness. In retirement at the house of a friend, near the gates of the city, he still occupied himself with his art, and alternated between the Violin and the Guitar. One day he seemed to revive, and performed a quartett of Beethoven, his particular favourite, with the greatest energy. Despite his extreme weakness, he went, some few days after, to hear a requiem for male voices, by Cherubini, finally, on the 21st of June, he attended in one of the churches at Marseilles, to take part in a solemn mass by Beethoven. However, the love of change, inherent in all valetudinarians, induced him to return to Genoa by sea, fully impressed that the voyage would recruit his health.

Vain hope! In the commencement of October of the same year, he wrote from his native city to M. Galafre, a painter, and an esteemed friend of his: "Being in much worse health than I was at Marseilles, I have resolved on passing the winter at Nice." Thus he believed he was flying from death, and death was pursuing him. Nice was destined to be his last abode. The progress of his malady was rapid—his voice became almost extinct, and dreadful fits of coughing, which daily became more frequent, finally reduced him to a shadow. The sinking of the features, a certain token of approaching death, was visible in his face. An Italian writer has furnished us with a most touching description of his last moments in the following terms:—

"On the last night of his existence, he appeared unusually tranquil. He had slept a little; when he awoke, he requested that the curtains of his bed should be drawn aside to contemplate the moon, which, at its full, was advancing calmly in the immensity of the pure heavens. While steadily gazing at this luminous orb, he again became drowsy, but the murmuring of the neighbouring trees awakened in his breast that sweet agitation which is the reality of the beautiful. At this solemn hour, he seemed desirous to return to Nature all the soft sensations which he was then possessed of; stretching forth his hands towards his enchanted Violin—to the faithful companion of his travels—to the magician which had robbed care of its stings—he sent to heaven, with its last sounds, the last sigh of a life which had been all melody."

The great artist expired the 27th of May, 1840, at the age of 56, leaving to his only son, Achille—the fruit of his liaison with the cantatrice, Antonia Bianchi, of Como—an immense fortune, and the title of Baron, which had been conceded to him in Germany. All had not ended with the man whose life was as extraordinary as his talent. Whether from the effect of certain popular rumours, of which mention will be made hereafter, or whether, from the fact of Paganini having died without receiving the last rites of the Church, he had left doubts as to his religion, his remains were refused interment in consecrated ground by the Bishop of Nice, Monsignor Antonio Galvano. Vainly did his son, his friends, and most of the artists of the city, solicit permission to celebrate a solemn service for his eternal rest, on the plea that, as in all cases of phthisis, the sufferer never believed his end was approaching, but had died suddenly; the Bishop remained inexorable, but proffered an authentic act of decease, with permission to remove the body wheresoever they pleased. This was not accepted, and the matter was brought before the tribunals. At Nice, a verdict was returned in favour of the Bishop. Recourse was then had to Rome, which remitted the Bishop's decision, and charged the Bishop of Turin, conjointly with two Canons of the Cathedral of Genoa, to institute an inquiry with reference to the catholicity of Paganini. All this time the body was lying in one of the rooms of the hospital at Nice; it was afterwards removed by sea from the lazaretto of Villa Franca, near the city, to a country spot named Polcevera, near Genoa, which belonged to the family of the illustrious artist. It was rumoured that piteous and extraordinary tones were heard there at night. To end these popular reports, the young Baron Paganini resolved on defraying the expense of a solemn service to the memory of his father, as Chevalier de St. George, which was celebrated at Parma in the church of the Steccata, belonging to that chivalrous order. After this ceremony, the friends of the deceased obtained permission from the Bishop of Parma to bring the body into the Duchy, to remove it to the Villa Gajona, and to inter it in the village church. This funeral homage was rendered to the remains of the celebrated man, in the month of May, 1845, but without pomp, in conformity with the orders which had emanated from the Government.

By his will, made on the 27th of April, 1837, and opened on the 1st of June, 1840, Paganini left to his son, legitimized by deeds of law, a fortune estimated at two millions (£80,000 sterling), out of which two legacies were to be paid, of fifty and sixty thousand francs, to his two sisters, leaving to the mother of his son Achille an annuity of 1,200 francs. Independently of his wealth, Paganini possessed a collection of valuable instruments, among which was an incomparable Stradiuari, estimated at upwards of 8,000 Austrian florins, a charming Guarnieri of the smaller pattern, an excellent Amati, a Stradiuari Bass, equally prized with his Violin of this master, and his large Guarnieri, the only instrument which accompanied him in his travels, and which he bequeathed to the town of Genoa, not being desirous that any artist should possess it after him.

The frenzied admiration which Paganini's prodigious talent excited wherever he went, and the wealth he amassed, were painfully compensated for, by the distressing state of his health during the greater part of his life. His biographers attribute this delicate state to the excesses of a stormy youth; but the immoderate use, during more than twenty years, of the quack medicine of Le Roy, exerted an equally fatal influence over his physical constitution. He rarely consulted the faculty, and less frequently followed their advice. His confidence in this favourite panacea was unshaken; he resorted to it on every occasion, convinced that no ill with which humanity is afflicted, could resist its action. The powerful agitation it excited was looked upon as a salutary crisis. Its frequent use subjected the intestinal functions to frequent disturbance, induced irritation, which became chronic, and produced nervous attacks, which often almost deprived him of the power of speech.

It was not only by his almost constant indisposition that Paganini expiated his glory and his success, for the malignity of his enemies pursued him for more than fifteen years with calumnious imputations, which everywhere left their traces, and compromised his honour. Crime was even imputed to him. The versions varied, as regards the deeds laid to his charge; according to one, his liaisons, unworthy of his talent, led him in his youth to the commission of highway robbery; others attributed to him a maddening and vindictive jealousy in love affairs, which frequently brought him to the verge of murder. Now his mistress, now his rival, had fallen victims to his irrepressible fury. It was even said, a long incarceration in prison had expiated his crime. The long intervals which took place between his concerts, either for the re-establishment of his health or for repose and meditation, favoured these calumnious reports. The qualities even of his talent were but weapons for his enemies, and it was said that the solitude of a prison, and the impossibility of replacing the strings of his Violin which had broken, led to his his marvellous performance on the fourth, the only one that remained upon his instrument. When Paganini visited Germany, France, and England, envy pursued him, greedy of collecting odious calumny, to oppose his success, as if it were decreed that genius and talent should ever expiate the advantages which nature and study had endowed them with. Paganini was frequently driven to defend himself in the columns of the press; vainly had he appealed to the testimony of the ambassadors of the foreign powers; vainly did he call upon his enemies to cite, with precision, the facts and dates which they had vaguely propagated; but no advantageous results were derived from this. Paris, especially, was hostile to him, although that city contributed principally to his fame. Apart from the real public, who entertain neither hatred nor prejudice, and who yield to the pleasure which talent provides for them, there is, in that city, a hunger-starved population, which exists on the ill it does and the good it prevents. This contemptible world speculated upon the celebrity of the artist, and persuaded itself that he would purchase their silence. Lithographic prints presented him a prisoner; journals attacked his morals, his humanity, his integrity. These reiterated attacks—this pillory to which he saw himself attached, as actor and as spectator—affected him deeply. He confided his sorrows to me, and took counsel from me, satisfying me perfectly of their unjust malice. I requested him to furnish me with some notes to enable me to write a letter, which I published with his signature, and was copied into most of the Paris journals. The facts, related in that letter, possess so much interest for the history of the most extraordinary man of our age, that I deem it important to give it a place here. I conceive it, besides, a duty to omit nothing that may avenge the calumnies which attached to one of the most dazzling glories of the musical art:—

"SIR,—So many proofs of kindness have been showered

upon me by the French public, so much encouraging approbation has been bestowed upon me, that I cannot avoid believing in the fame which it is said preceded me in Paris, and that I fell not short of my reputation at my concerts. But, if any doubt of that kind existed in my bosom, it would be removed by the eagerness evinced by your artists to produce my likeness, and by the great number of portraits of Paganini—faithful resemblances or not—which cover the walls of your city; but, sir, it is not only simple portraits that speculators of that nature stop at—for, while walking yesterday on the Boulevard des Italiens, I saw in a shop, where engravings are sold, a lithograph representing Paganini in prison. 'Oh!' I exclaimed, 'here are some honest folks who, after the fashion of Basile, make a profit out of certain calumnies which have pursued me for the last fifteen years.' However, I examined laughingly this mystification, with all the details that the imagination of the artist had conjured up, when I perceived that a large number of persons had congregated around me, each of whom, confronting my face with that of the young man represented in the lithograph, verified the change that had taken place in my person since my detention. I then saw that it was looked on in a serious light by those you call, I believe, louts, and that the speculation was a good one. It struck me that, as everybody must live, I might furnish the artists, who are kind enough to consider me worthy of their attention, with some anecdotes—anecdotes from which they could derive subjects of similar facetiæ to the subject in question. It is to give them publicity, that I claim from your kindness the insertion of this letter in the 'Revue Musicale.'

"They have represented me in prison; but they are ignorant of the cause of my incarceration; however, they know as much of that as I do myself, and those who concocted the anecdote. There are many stories in reference to this, which would supply them with as many subjects for their pencils; for example, it is stated that, having found a rival in my mistress' apartment, I stabbed him honourably in the back, while he was unable to defend himself. Others assert, that, in the madness of jealousy,

I slew my mistress; but they do not state how I effected my bloody purpose. Some assert I used a dagger—others that, desirous of witnessing her agony, I used poison. Each has settled it in accordance with his own fancy. Why should not lithographers have the same privilege? I will relate what occurred to me at Padua, nearly fifteen years since. I had played at a concert with great success. The next day, seated at the table d'hôte (I was the sixtieth) my entrance in the room passed unobserved. One of the guests spoke of the great effect I had produced the previous evening. His neighbour concurred in all that was said, and added, 'There is nothing surprising in Paganini's performance—he acquired his talent while confined in a dungeon during eight years, having only his Violin to soften the rigours of his confinement. He was condemned for having, coward-like, stabbed one of my friends, who was his rival.' As you may imagine, every one was shocked by the enormity of my crime. I then addressed myself to the person who was so well acquainted with my history, and requested to know when and where this had taken place. Every eye was directed towards me. Judge the surprise when they recognised the principal actor in this tragical history! The narrator was embarrassed. It was no longer his friend who had been assassinated. He heard—it had been affirmed—he believed; but it was not improbable he had been deceived. This is how an artist's reputation is trifled with, because indolent people will never comprehend that one may study at liberty as well as under lock and key.

"A still more ridiculous report, at Vienna, tested the credulity of some enthusiasts. I had played the variations entitled "Le Streghe" (the Witches), and they produced some effect. One individual, who was represented to me as of a sallow complexion, melancholy air, and bright eye, affirmed that he saw nothing surprising in my performance, for he had distinctly seen, while I was playing my variations, the devil at my elbow directing my arm and guiding my bow. My resemblance to him was a proof of my origin. He was clothed in red—had horns on his head—and carried his tail between his legs. After so minute a description, you will understand, sir, it was impossible to doubt the fact; hence, many concluded they had discovered the secret of what they termed my wonderful feats.

"My mind was disturbed for a long time by these reports, and I sought every means to prove their absurdity. I remarked that from the age of fourteen, I had continued to give concerts, consequently was always before the public; that I had been engaged as leader of the orchestra, and musical director to the Court of Lucca; that if it were true, I had been detained eight years in prison, for having assassinated my mistress or my rival, it must have taken place before my appearance in public; that I must have had a mistress and a rival at seven years of age. At Vienna I appealed to the ambassador of my country, who declared he had known me for upwards of twenty years as an honest man, and I succeeded in setting the calumny aside temporarily; but there are always some remains, and I was not surprised to find them here. How am I to act, sir? I see nothing but resignation, and submit to the malignity which exerts itself at my expense. I deem it, however, a duty, before I conclude, to communicate to you an anecdote, which gave rise to the injurious reports propagated against me. A violinist, of the name of Duranowski, who was at Milan in 1798, connected himself with two persons of disreputable character, and was induced to accompany them to a village, where they purposed assassinating the priest, who was reported to be very rich. Fortunately, the heart of one failed him at the moment of the dreadful deed, and he immediately denounced his accomplices. The gendarmerie soon arrived on the spot, and took Duranowski and his companion prisoners at the moment they arrived at the priest's house. They were condemned to the galleys for twenty years, and thrown into a dungeon; but General Menou, after he became Governor of Milan, restored Duranowski to liberty, after two years' detention. Will you credit it?—upon this groundwork they have constructed my history. It was necessary that the violinist should end in *i*, it was Paganini; the assassination became that of my mistress or my rival; and I it was who was sent to prison,—with this exception, that I was to discover there a new school for the Violin: the irons were not adjudged against me, in order that my arms might be at perfect liberty. Since these reports are persisted in, against all probability, I must necessarily bear them with resignation. One hope remains: it is, that after my death, calumny will abandon its prey, and that those who have so cruelly avenged my triumphs, will leave my ashes at rest.—Receive, &c.,

"PAGANINI."

As just stated, Paganini was deeply mortified by these reports which affected his honour. He wrote to the editors of the journals in Vienna; and when Mr. Schottky, of Prague, formed the project of writing his biography, to crush his calumniators, Paganini, who rejoiced at the idea of such a publication, urged his friend to hasten his labours. He wrote to him from Berlin:—"It is high time I should write to you. I have no bad news to communicate, though I suffer slightly with my eyes, which inconveniences me a good deal. You have probably seen the Dresden journals. I met with all kinds of gratifications at Dresden, which the extreme kindness of the royal family completed. It is true, I learned that you had in one of your contributions promised my biography, but I have not heard anything since. My curiosity is at its utmost pitch. My relation, of whom I spoke to you, joined me at Dresden; he is also extremely anxious. Do let us see some portion of your work. My honour is in your keeping. How fortunate to have found an avenger, whose name alone suffices to crush the basest calumnies! Your integrity and your talents will drive my enemies to despair, and to you will remain the gratification of having done a generous action."

Nothing can be more honourable or more natural than the indignation felt by Paganini at the calumnies which his success engendered; but it would seem that he was deceived as to the means of silencing them: for the publication of the chronological order of his life would easily have demonstrated the absurdity of the reports propagated against him. It is a fact, that until he was nearly fifteen years of age, he remained under the paternal roof. Hence he proceeded to Lucca, where he unfortunately formed an acquaintance with some disreputable persons, who, taking advantage of his inexperience, robbed him of the fruits of his industry, and drove him to Pisa, Arezzo, and Leghorn, where he gave concerts to repair the inroads his losses had made, and improve his pecuniary position. He was at this latter place in 1801, and was then only seventeen years of age. This date is authentically established by Gervasoni, who was his contemporary. Some months after, his predilection for the Violin changed, and he took up the Guitar, acquired a mastery over that instrument nearly equal to the Violin, and wrote for it several distinguished compositions, which are still sought for in Italy. In 1804, we find him at Genoa, giving instructions to the young Catarina Calcagno, who became a most worthy pupil. The following year, he enters the service at the Court of Lucca, remains in that town until 1808, then undertakes a professional tour, arrives at Leghorn, and plays at several concerts. In 1809, Blangini meets him at Turin. In the same year he returns to Florence, where Bartolini executes his bust. In 1810, he travels through the Romagna, and performs particularly at Rimini, an inhabitant of which furnished an account to M. Conestabile. It is afterwards that his adventure at Ferrara occurs; and the 16th of August of the following year he gives concerts at Parma, as confirmed by M. Gervasoni. Returning to Florence, he remains there during 1812, where, at the beginning of 1813, the affair takes place which drives him from Court. In the same year he gives thirteen concerts at Milan. In 1814 he is at Genoa, his native place. He then returns to Milan, gives eleven concerts there, and proceeds to Bologna, where he meets Rossini. In 1815, he makes his second professional tour in Romagna, and plays at Ancona, returning again to his native place. In March, 1816, he goes to hear Lafont at Milan, receives the challenge, gives concerts, and proceeds to Venice in the summer of the same year. He remains there nearly a year, according to the report of a correspondent of the "Leipziger Musikalische Zeitung," from which period until his death the public journals teem with accounts of his brilliant successes. It is manifest, and beyond contradiction, that during an existence constantly before the public, no period can be found where he could have suffered a detention of eight years, or even the time necessary for undergoing a criminal procedure. Paganini, with the design of confounding his vilifiers, should have collected the testimonies of those he had known previously to and during all this period, and have published the chronological table which has been thus sketched: the whole matter would then have been set at rest.

Human credulity is prone to feed on outrageous absurdities. Not only was his dignity as a man attacked, for endeavours were ever made to deprive him of this, and to grant him only a fantastic existence. The almost insuperable difficulties he had overcome as a violinist, were not the only motives which gave birth to the reports circulated. The extraordinary expression of his face, his livid paleness, his dark and penetrating eye, together with the sardonic smile which occasionally played upon his lips, appeared to the vulgar, and to certain diseased minds, unmistakable evidences of satanic origin. It has been seen by his letter, which has been given *in extenso*, what he himself related on that subject. But these ridiculous ideas were not entertained in Germany only, for there are traces of them even in Italy, and they probably had some effect upon the difficulties which attended his obsequies. M. Amati, a distinguished writer, has furnished M. Schottky with an anecdote which has reference to his acquaintance with Paganini at Florence. It will be seen what impression the extraordinary aspect of this singular being had upon nervous temperaments. Thus speaks the narrator:—"Near the gate of Pitti, at Florence, there is a steep hill, on the summit of which stands the ancient Fiesole, formerly the rival of the capital of Tuscany, but divested of its former splendour. Here the purest air is inhaled, and the beauty of the prospect produces rather the effect of a dream than of reality. One beautiful May morning, when the flowers and verdure lay smiling, kissed by the sun's rays, and all nature was beaming with youth, I ascended this hill by its most rugged path, from whence the most beautiful view is obtained. In front of me was a stranger, who, from time to time, stopped to recover his breath, and admire the enchanting landscape, which met his eye in every direction. Insensibly I approached him. Believing himself alone, he spoke aloud, and accompanied his monologue with rapid gesticulations and loud laughter. Suddenly he checked himself; his lynx-like eye had perceived in the distance a charming object, which soon after also attracted my attention. It was a young peasant girl, who was approaching towards us slowly, carrying a basket of flowers. She wore a straw hat; her hair, dark and lustrous as jet, played upon her forehead; and the regularity of her handsome features was softened by the mildness of her looks. With a beautifully formed hand she constantly replaced her shining ringlets, which the refreshing zephyr displaced. The stranger, astonished at so much beauty, fixed his ardent looks upon her; when she had got near to him, she seemed transfixed at the appearance of the individual who stood before her, grew pale, and trembled. Her basket seemed ready to fall from her hands. She, however, hurried on, and soon disappeared behind a projection. During this period, I contemplated the stranger, whose eyes were fixed in the direction the girl had taken. Never had I seen so extraordinary a face. He merely cast upon me a passing glance, accompanied by a most singular smile, and pursued his way.

"The next day, dark clouds, driven by the winds, rolled along like the sea waves; scarcely was the sun visible, yet, despite the weather, I went out, and having traversed the bridge Delle Grazie, outside the gate which bears that name, I directed my steps to the right, towards the hill, on the summit of which I already perceived the ruined castle with its drawbridge. I approached the remains of this ancient edifice, through the dilapidated walls of which the wind was whistling. Here everything bore the impress of destruction. Here, contemplating the fearful ravages of time, and listening to the mournful melodies of the hurricane, the moanings of a human voice struck upon my ear, and made me shudder. It seemed as if the voice proceeded from a subterranean cavity near which I was standing. I rushed forward to its mouth, where I found a man—pale and with haggard looks, lying upon the moss. I recognised the stranger of the previous day; his searching look was fixed upon me; I recoiled from it, and perceiving the stranger was in no need of assistance, I withdrew.

"On the following evening, I was walking by the side of the Arno, the moonlight flickering as it rose. The nightingale's note, and the warbling of birds of every kind preparing to roost, were saluting the departing rays of day. Sounds of a totally different nature suddenly intermingled with these harmonized melodies of nature. Attracted by this exquisite and unknown music, I followed the direction from whence they seemed to proceed, and I again found myself near the singular being who had occupied all my thoughts for the last three days. Carelessly lying beneath a tree, his features were now as calm as they had appeared troubled the day previous, and as he listened with impassioned expression to the fury of the tempest in the old castle, so did he now seem to enjoy the concert of the feathered tribe, whose notes he was whistling with most astounding imitation. I could not explain the strange destiny that led me constantly into his presence.

"My astonishment had not yet ceased, for, on returning the following evening from a long walk, just as the stars began their first scintillations, I sat down to repose myself under the Loggie degli Uffizi. A joyous party passed me, and sat down on a marble seat some distance from me; soon after, celestial sounds struck upon my ear, by turns joyful and plaintive, evidently produced by the hand of a superior artist. Silence succeeded to the hilarious shouts of the merry party, all of whom seemed as transfixed by the divine music as I was myself. They all rose, silently, to follow the artist, who continued walking while he played. I also followed, to discover what instrument it was I heard, and who the artist might be that discoursed so enchantingly upon it. Arrived at the square of the Palazzo Vecchio, the party entered a restaurant. I followed them. Here they regained their former merriment, and the leader, more than his companions, displayed extraordinary animation. To my great surprise, the instrument was a guitar (which seemed to have become magical), and the performer, I discovered to be the stranger I had so continuously met. He was no longer the suffering being he had seemed: his eyes beamed, his veins swelled with exultation, his coat and waistcoat were both unbuttoned, his cravat loosened, and his gesticulations those of a madman. I inquired his name. 'None of us knows it,' replied the individual, one of the party, to whom I addressed myself; 'I was in company with my friends, who were singing and dancing to my guitar, when this singular man pushed in among us, and snatching the guitar from my hands, commenced playing without saying a word. Annoyed at the intrusion, we were about to lay hands upon him, but without noticing us in the least, he continued playing, subjugating us by his exquisite performance. Each time we inquired his name, he resumed his playing without making any reply. He occasionally ceased for a while, to relate to us some extraordinary anecdote. In this manner he has brought us hither, without more knowledge of him than you possess.'

"Some days after, Paganini was announced to give a concert. Eager to hear the incomparable artist, whose fame was so universal, and whom I had not yet heard, I went to the theatre, which was literally crowded to suffocation. The utmost impatience was manifested until the concert commenced with a symphony, which, although by a composer of eminence, was listened to with indifference. At last the artist appeared. I was astonished at recognising in him the stranger who had so mystified me for some days, whom I had met at Fiesole, etc. I will not attempt to describe the effect his performance produced—the transports of frenzy his incomparable talent excited. Let it suffice to say, that on that one evening, he seemed to conjoin all the delightful impressions of the graceful appearance of the peasant girl of the mountain, the hurricane in the ruins, the warbling of the feathered songsters on the banks of the Arno, and the inspiring delirium of the evening at the Loggie."

With a people so imaginative as the Italians, so extraordinary a looking person as Paganini, his wondrous talent, and the eccentricity of his mode of life, naturally conduced to superstitious ideas, and the belief in the supernatural. Many believed he had entered into a compact with the devil. In Germany these prejudices were greater even than among the Italians. It has been seen in his letter already given what was said of him at Vienna, when he played his variations on the "Witches' Dance." At Leipzig, the "Zeitung für die elegant Welt" gave the following account of one of his concerts:—"In the Hotel de Pologne, resided a lady of exceeding beauty, whose tresses were the object of much admiration, but whose features wore an aspect of deep melancholy, though a sweet yet sad smile was ever playing on her lips. I had seen her once: this sufficed to imprint her features upon my memory, and I sought every means to see her at all times. The evening Paganini gave his last concert, I was near the stage, and although my eyes wandered all over the theatre, I did not discover her I sought so anxiously. Paganini appeared. Can I describe the magic of his bow? The marvellous tones he extracted from the melancholy and plaintive G string touched every heart; and upon this occasion more so than I ever remember. At this moment, the sound of a sigh, such as proceeds from some person dying, struck upon my ear. I looked around, and I saw my *incognita*, white as marble, unconscious, apparently, of the tears which fell in showers down her cheeks. I uttered a cry of surprise, which was heard throughout the theatre; every voice being at the time hushed into silence. Paganini, who was only a few paces from me, turned round and looked at me. An extraordinary smile, such as I had never before seen, played upon his face; but it did not seem either intended for me or the lady. I watched its direction, and perceived, not without emotion, dressed in the English fashion, and seated next the lady, my not very reputable acquaintance of Elbingerode, who returned the smile with one no less extraordinary. They were then intimate? I understand that smile now. In reality, it had been generally observed, and for a long time surmised, that Paganini and Satan were most intimately connected, or that they were one and the same person. My discovery made me forget my lady; but judge of my horror, when upon turning round I saw her neighbour take her hand, squeeze it with affection, and the lady grow paler than before. I was thunderstruck; but at this moment the applause increased. Paganini had finished playing. The audience rose, as did the lady and her friend. I followed them to the door, before which stood a carriage with two black horses. The lady got in, followed by her cavalier, when the carriage flew off, bright flashes of lightning bursting forth from the horses' eyes. Greatly agitated, I returned to the theatre; but Paganini's marvels no longer astounded me. The concert concluded, I left by the same door through which the mysterious lady had passed, and then found there was no place where a carriage could stand."

Paganini was deeply affected by these rumours, which not only detracted from his position, but tended to render his talent valueless. It is not improbable that in his youth he had himself contributed to the propagation of such fabrications by his eccentricities. But when age crept on—when honours and successes had accumulated—he discovered that none, however great his fame, however favoured by fortune, could be great when general esteem is withheld. With the view of ending the ridiculous reports concerning his origin, he published at Prague the following letter, which his mother had written to him on the 21st of July, 1828:—

"Dearest Son,—At last, after seven months have elapsed since I wrote to you at Milan, I had the happiness of receiving your letter of the 9th current, through the intermediary of Signor Agnino, and was much rejoiced to find that you were in the enjoyment of good health. I am also delighted to find that, after your travels to Paris and London, you purpose visiting Genoa expressly to embrace me. I assure you, my prayers are daily offered up to the Most High, that my health may be sustained, also yours, so that my desire may be realized.

"My dream has been fulfilled, and that which God promised me has been accomplished. Your name is great, and art, with the help of God, has placed you in a position of independence. Beloved, esteemed by your fellow citizens, you will find in my bosom and those of your friends, that repose which your health demands.

"The portraits which accompanied your letter have given me great pleasure. I had seen in the papers all the accounts you give me of yourself. You may imagine, as your mother, what an infinite source of joy it was to me. Dear son, I entreat you to continue to inform me of all that concerns you, for with this assurance I shall feel that it will prolong my days, and be convinced that I shall still have the happiness of embracing you.

"We are all well. In the name of all your relations, I thank you for the sums of money you have sent. Omit nothing that will render your name immortal. Eschew the vices of great cities, remembering that you have a mother who loves you affectionately, and whose fondest aspirations are your health and happiness. She will never cease her supplications to the All-powerful for your preservation.

"Embrace your amiable companion for me, and kiss little Achille. Love me as I love you.

"Your ever affectionate mother,

"TERESA PAGANINI."

This letter was not necessary to prove to reasoning mortals that the great artist was not a son of Satan. But the ignorant mass listens not to reason, nor are its superstitious beliefs easily removed. Opinion in France did justice to these follies, but they seemed to revive afterwards, and acquired renewed strength after the decease of him who had been so calumniated during his life.

Nothing could be more variable than the moral dispositions of Paganini; at one time melancholy and taciturn, passing several hours seated, without uttering a word; at another, he would give himself entirely up to unrestrained gaiety, without any apparent motive for either the one or the other. He seldom spoke much;

but while travelling, the movement of the carriage rendered him loquacious. Mr. George Harrys, who lived for some time on terms of intimacy with him, and who has published some curious details on his private life,* states that his bad health rendered his speaking aloud extremely painful, but when the noise of the wheels rattling over the stones was almost deafening, he spoke loudly and rapidly. It was not, as with most persons, the beauty of the country through which he passed that made him communicative, for he paid no attention to the lovely landscapes which met his eye in every direction; rapid transit seemed to be his only aim; but there was something in the rolling of the coach which made conversation a necessity. His constant suffering did not permit him to enjoy a beautiful country, where others dwelt who were blessed with health. Besides, he was always cold, and even at a summer heat of twenty-two degrees he wrapped his large cloak around him, and ensconced himself in a corner of a carriage, with the windows hermetically closed. By a singular contradiction, he invariably kept all the windows of his apartments wide open, to take, as he called it, an air bath. He cursed the climate of Germany, of France, and above all of England, saying there was no living but in Italy. Travelling was exceedingly painful to him, suffering, as he constantly did, from pain in the abdomen; hence his wish to travel quickly. In the agony he experienced, his habitual paleness was replaced by a livid and greenish hue. Sleep to him was a source of great delight, and he would sleep uninterruptedly for two or three hours consecutively, and awake full of cheerfulness. When the horses were being changed, he either remained in the carriage, or walked about until the fresh horses were put to; but he never entered an inn or post-house until he arrived at the end of his journey. Before starting, he neither took tea nor coffee, but a basin of soup, or a cup of chocolate. If he started early in the morning, he would do so fasting, and frequently remained

* Paganini in seinem Reisewagen und Zimmer, etc. Aus einem Reisejournale. Brunswick, 1830. 12mo.

nearly the whole day without taking any refreshment. His luggage caused no trouble, as it consisted only of a small dilapidated trunk, containing his precious Guarnieri Violin, his jewels, his money, and a few fine linen articles, a carpet bag, and a hat-case, which was placed in the interior of the carriage. Careless of all that related to the comforts of life, he was alike negligent in his toilet. A small napkin would contain his entire wardrobe; his papers, which were of paramount importance, representing immense value, he kept in a small red pocket-book, which also contained his accounts. None but himself could decipher these hieroglyphics of his Babel-like accounts, where pell-mell were mixed up Vienna and Carlsruhe, Berlin, Frankfort, and Leipzig, receipts and outlay for post-horses, etc., and concert tickets. All was clear to him; though extremely ignorant of arithmetic, he had devised certain means of arriving at an exact account of all his affairs.

In the inns on the road, Paganini was never dissatisfied. It was a matter of indifference to him, whether he was shown into a garret or an elegantly-furnished chamber, whether the bed was good or bad, as long as he was removed from all noise. "I have enough noise in large towns," he would say, "I wish to rest on the road." His supper was always extremely light; frequently he would take nothing but a cupful of camomile tea, after which he would sleep soundly till the morning. However, when, about fifteen years before his death, he was attacked with the phthisis which ultimately proved fatal, a convulsive cough frequently interrupted his sleep; but as soon as the crisis was over, he was asleep again.

The most securely-guarded state prisoner never experienced so monotonous a course of existence as that to which Paganini condemned himself at home; he left his room with regret, and only seemed happy in perfect solitude. Many have thought his Violin occupied him constantly. Never was error greater—he never touched it except to tune it previously to going to a rehearsal or a concert. "I have laboured enough to acquire my talent," he would say, "it is time I should rest myself." The anecdote is perhaps known, of an Englishman, a passionate admirer and amateur of the Violin, who, intent on discovering the secret of the great artist's study, followed in his steps for more than six months, staying at the same hotels, and always when possible in the next room. Vainly, however, did he seek to hear him study some of his difficulties—the most profound silence reigned in the artist's apartment. It occurred, however, that on one occasion the rooms of the amateur and the artist were only separated by a door which was not used. Peeping through the keyhole, the curiosity of the amateur was, as it appeared, about to be gratified. He saw Paganini, seated on a sofa, taking from its case the precious Violin, which, on being raised to his shoulder, assured him his long-sought happiness was about to be realized; but not a note was heard, for Paganini merely moved his left hand up and down the finger-board, to calculate certain positions, without using the bow. This done, the Violin was replaced in its case. In utter despair, the Englishman gave up the fruitless pursuit, and returned to England.

Paganini did not seek to conceal that his constant study of the instrument in his early years precluded his attending to his education, and that his mind was but ill-stored with literary instruction. He never looked into a book, not even to wile away any portion of time by reading a romance. History and the sciences were sealed books to him. M. Schottky, notwithstanding, found among the documents which were furnished to him by M. Amati, an anecdote which indicates that the great violinist's memory retained certain smatterings of history, mythology, and poetry, which he would apply occasionally most oppositely. Dining one day with the celebrated poets, Monti and Ugo Foscolo, at the residènce of the beautiful, rich, and witty Comtesse F——'s, Foscolo, who was captivated with the charms of the Comtesse, arrived the last, and finding Monti, his rival, addressing her in terms of gallantry, he abruptly quitted the apartment, and hastened to allay his fierceness on the garden terrace. Here he met Paganini, and his passion subsided. Approaching him with great warmth, and seizing his hand, he said to him, "When I heard you at the concert yesterday, Homer stood before me in all his sublimity. The grandeur of the first movement of your concerto brought to my mind the arrival of the Greek ships before Troy. The exquisite loveliness of the Adagio pictured to me the tender love-talk of Achilles and Briséis. When will you let me hear the despair and wailings of the hero over the body of Patroclus?" Paganini replied, without hesitation, "When Achilles Paganini finds his Patroclus among violinists."

Political events had no interest for him; he consequently never read a newspaper unless it contained something concerning himself. His whole thoughts were occupied on projects for the future. Among these were the founding of a musical conservatory in Italy, the publication of his compositions, the writing of operas, and abandoning his professional tours. While dwelling on these subjects, he would pace his room with great rapidity, arrange his stray pieces of music, or number his red diary, dress himself and go to dinner, or have it brought to his room, which he preferred to the *table d'hôte*. He spent a great portion of the day reclining on his bed, and left his room only in the evening, to walk for about an hour. He would pass the entire evening without light in his apartment, and rarely went to bed later than half-past ten. He frequently remained for hours absorbed in deep thought, almost motionless. Mistrustful, like most Italians, he complained of the treachery of some of his most intimate friends, which necessarily rendered him the more so; hence his dislike to society—he did not believe he could repose the slightest confidence in any one.

Notwithstanding his extreme repugnance to receiving visits, his world-wide fame brought sometimes from sixty to eighty visitors, anxious to see and speak with him; many of these he would refer to his secretary, but others he could not avoid receiving. Circumspect with those who came on business, he was more so with artists who came to discover the secret of his talent; he listened to these patiently. His fatigue was so great after receiving these visits, that he would bolt his door, and not answer anyone who knocked.

The invitations he received for dinners and suppers were very numerous in all the towns he visited, or remained in to give concerts; they annoyed him, and he refused most of them, aware of his habit of partaking of everything that was placed on the table. He could eat and drink largely without feeling any ill effects at the time, but in a day or two his intestinal pains would come on with redoubled force. He would invariably, if he could do so without being observed, retire to rest as soon as he left the table. He was infinitely gayer previous to dinner than after. One would be inclined to suppose he was desirous of impressing upon his host the sacrifice he made in accepting the invitation: it was so, in fact.

At evening parties he was extremely cheerful, if no mention was made of music; but if, with the ill-judged view of affording him amusement, it was proposed or spoken of, his spirits immediately left him. If to gather his opinions upon other violinists, or to question him upon his talent, he only replied monosyllabically, and endeavoured to avoid the inquisition by stealing away to another part of the room, or to interrupt the conversation by observations on other subjects. In the large cities of Germany, vocal and instrumental societies deemed it a homage to his talent to perform before him some musical compositions; but, although he would appear to listen with attention, his mind was pre-occupied on other subjects, and he rarely knew what he listened to. He occasionally avowed, with great sincerity, that the obligation of identifying his public existence with music made him feel an imperious desire to forget the art when he entered into ordinary life. Nor can it be dissimulated that this idiosyncracy pertains to almost every artist who has obtained great celebrity, and who has acquired popular fame. With these, all their faculties are concentrated in the feeling of their personality. Art, separated from their own glorification, does not exist. Gluck and Grétry recognized no music but their own, nor believed any other to be worthy of being performed. How many composers have been imbued with the same feeling, differing with those great men only in dissimulation! With those whose executive talents bring them in contact with the public, it is worse still; without personal ovations, it is not only indifference for the art, it is hatred. Hence, when, having returned to the ordinary conditions of life, and withdrawn from the manifestations of enthusiasm they have for so long a period excited, artists who come into this category decline rapidly, and present in their old age a spectacle of moral degradation, unless, by an extraordinary exception, great intellectual faculties have been united to their extraordinary talent.

Paganini felt great pleasure in a small circle of friends, and in quiet conversation. The amusements of society delighted him; and he would remain until a late hour, where he did not appear to be an object of attention. He did not like the glare of light—his sight having been affected by stage lights—hence his habit of playing with his back to the lights, and of remaining in the dark when at home. His memory was excellent, despite his habitual abstraction. When once persons had been introduced to him, their features and names were never forgotten; but, by some inexplicable singularity, he never remembered the name of a town in which he gave concerts the moment he left it.

Notwithstanding the enormous number of concerts he gave, Paganini was pre-occupied the day on which one was given. He would remain idle the whole morning, lying on a sofa. Before going to a rehearsal, he would open his Violin-case to examine the state of his strings, tune it, and prepare the orchestral parts of the pieces he intended playing. During these operations he took large quantities of snuff—a certain token with him of great mental excitement and disquietude. On arriving at rehearsal, his first care was to see that no person was in the room or theatre. Should any one be there, he merely indicated to the band what he desired by almost an imperceptible sound, or slight pizzicato. He was extremely severe with the band; and would have a solo or a tutti repeated for the slightest error. If this continued, he would pace to and fro before the orchestra, and dart the most furious looks at the musicians; but when a tutti came in too soon, before the termination of a cadenza, he burst forth into a tempest of rage which would cause the boldest to tremble. When, however, the accompaniment was satisfactory, he would smile, and express his approbation aloud, in these words, "Bravissimo! Siete tutti virtuosi!" When he came to a pause for the introduction of a cadenza, the musicians all rose, eager to observe what he was about to play, but Paganini would merely play a few notes—stop suddenly—and, turning towards them, would laughingly add, "Et cætera, Messieurs!" It was only in the evening he would put forth all his strength. After the rehearsal, he would converse for a few moments with the leader, to thank him for the attention that had been paid, and sought out especial passages for his particular observation. He invariably carried away himself the orchestral parts, of which he was particularly careful. The principal part was never seen, as he played from memory, to avoid his pieces being copied. When he returned home he partook of a light repast, threw himself upon his bed, and remained there until the carriage came to take him to the theatre. A few minutes sufficed for his toilet, and he proceeded at once to the concert. When he arrived he evinced as much gaiety, as he had displayed gravity during the day. His first question was "is there a large audience?" If answered in the affirmative, he would say, "good—good! excellent people!" if, on the contrary, he was told the audience was small, he expressed a fear that the effect of the music would be lost in the empty boxes.

Paganini was not always alike disposed for his concerts. He had doubts of himself; and, trying several difficult passages, if he failed in executing them with his usual facility, he became angry, and exclaimed, "If I were in Paris, I would not play to-day." He would frequently recover himself during the evening, and say ingeniously to his friends, "I have played better at the end than at the commencement of the concert." He kept the public waiting a long time before he came on. His departure from the theatre resembled a triumph; a crowd formed an avenue to his carriage, and greeted him with loud acclamations; he was received similarly on his arrival at his hotel. Paganini seemed delighted with the homage, and frequently mixed with the crowds that surrounded the doors. He would join the company at the *table d'hôte* in the best possible spirits, and would sup heartily.

There are few examples of such devotion to severe study as Paganini evinced in the accomplishment of his art. He created the difficulties he performed, with a view of varying the effects and augmenting the resources of his instrument—this, as it is seen, having been his object, so soon as he was capable of reflecting on his ultimate destiny. Having played the music of the old masters, particularly that of Pugnani, Viotti and Kreutzer, he felt he could never attain great fame if he followed in their path. Chance brought under his notice the ninth work of Locatelli, entitled, "l'Arte di Nuova Modulazione," and he at once saw in it a new world of ideas and facts, though, on its first appearance it was unsuccessful from its excessive difficulty, and, perhaps, also, because it was in advance of the period when "classic" forms should be departed from. Circumstances were favourable to Paganini, for the necessity of innovation was at its zenith in his day. In adopting the ideas of his predecessors, in resuscitating forgotten effects, in superadding what his genius and perseverance gave birth to, he arrived at that distinctive character of performance and his ultimate greatness. The diversity of sounds—the different methods of tuning his instrument—the frequent employment of double and single harmonic notes—the simultaneous pizzicato and bow passages—the various staccati — the use of the double and even triple notes — a prodigious facility in executing wide intervals with unerring precision, joined to an extraordinary number of various styles of bowing—such were the principal features of Paganini's talent — means which were rendered perfect by his execution — his exquisite nervous sensibility, and his enormous musical feeling. From the manner in which he placed himself, leaning, as it were, on his hip, from the position of his right arm, and the manner in which he held his bow, it would have been thought its movements would be nothing less than awkward, and the arm all stiffness; but it was soon observed that the bow and the arm moved with equal ease, and what appeared to be the result of some malformation, was the result of deep study of that which was most favourable to the effect the artist wished to produce. His bow was of ordinary dimensions; but was screwed up with more than usual tension. It is probable Paganini found it preferable for his bounding staccato, which differed from that of all other violinists. In the notice which he wrote at Lucca, he says great surprise was manifested at the length of his bow, and the thickness of his strings; but, some time after, he evidently discovered the difficulty of producing vibration in every part of the strings, and consequently, of obtaining a perfect tone, for he gradually diminished their dimensions—and when he played in Paris his strings were under the medium size. Paganini's hands were large, dry, and nervous. His fingers, by dint of excessive practice, had acquired a suppleness and aptitude difficult to conceive. The thumb of the left hand fell easily upon the palm of his hand, when necessary for the execution of certain shifting passages.

The quality of tone which Paganini brought from his instrument was clear and pure, without being excessively full, except in certain effects, when it was manifest he collected all his power to arrive at extraordinary results. But what most distinguished this portion of his talent was the variety of voices he drew from the strings, by means of his own, or which, after having been discovered by others, had been neglected, their full import having been misunderstood. Thus, the harmonic sounds, which before his time had only been considered as curious and limited effects, rather than as a positive benefit to a violinist, formed an important feature in Paganini's performance. It was not only for an isolated effect that he employed them, but as an artificial means to reach certain intervals, which the largest hand could never embrace. It was from the harmonic sounds that he obtained on the fourth string a compass of three octaves. Before Paganini, none had imagined that beyond natural harmonics, it was possible to execute thirds, fifths, sixths; in fact, that at the octaves in diatonic succession, natural and harmonic sounds could be produced. All these Paganini executed in every position with the utmost facility. In singing he frequently produced a vibratory effect, which greatly resembled the human voice, but when, by sliding the hand, the voice became like that of an old woman, the effect was affected and exaggerated. Paganini's intonation was perfect; this rare quality was not the least of the advantages he possessed over other violinists.

After having spoken of the great qualities of Paganini's talent, it is necessary to consider it from the general impression it produced upon the public. Many overleap the bounds of reason in expatiating on the poetry of his playing, particularly upon his singing. He was cited as the great Violin singer—as the creator of a pathetic and dramatic school, applied to the art of bowing. I confess that I do not look at his prodigious talent in this light. What I experienced in listening to him was astonishment—unbounded admiration; but I was seldom moved by that feeling which appears to me inseparable from the true expression of music. The poetry of the great violinist consisted, principally, in his brilliancy; and, if I may be allowed the expression, the mastery of his bow. There was fulness and grandeur in his phrasing—but there was no tenderness in his accents. In the prayer from "Mosè," for example, he was great when the baritone voice was heard on the fourth string, from the elevated character he gave to it; but when he came to the part of Elcia, an octave higher on the same string, he fell into an affected strain of heavy, tremulous sounds, which good taste would have rejected. His triumph was in the last major strain; here he was sublime—and he then left an impression bordering on enthusiasm.

To pronounce judgment upon Paganini, it was necessary to hear him in his own especial style—that which most characterized his talent. In his concerts in Paris, he thought it necessary to flatter the national feeling by playing a concerto by Kreutzer and one by Rode—but he scarcely rose above mediocrity in their performance. His secretary, Mr. Harrys, tells us the opinion Paganini formed of himself as regards these attempts. He said to him, "I have my own peculiar style; in accordance with this, I regulate my composition. To play those of other artists, I must arrange them accordingly: I had much rather write a piece in which I can trust myself entirely to my own musical impressions." The unfavourable impression he made in Paris, with these two pieces, was a lesson to him; he never played from that time any music but his own. Paganini's art did not apply to any species of composition—his was a specialty, of which he alone could be the interpreter—an art born with him, the secret of which he has carried with him to the grave.

I have used a word he often repeated—for he frequently insisted that his talent resulted from a secret discovered by him—and which he would reveal before his death, in a "study for the Violin," that should only contain a small number of pages, but that should cause the utmost consternation to all violinists. He cited, in support of the infallibility of his secret, the experiment that he had made at Naples, upon a violoncellist of little talent, named Gaetano Ciandelli, who, by the revelation of the mystery, became transformed in one morning into a *virtuoso.* Apart from the study of mechanism—for which there is no substitute—no secret can exist from talent, but that which nature implants in the heart of the artist; there is, however, something astounding and mysterious in the faculty which Paganini possessed, of invariably overcoming the almost unheard-of difficulties, without ever touching the Violin except at concerts and rehearsals. Mr. Harrys, who was his secretary, and did not leave him for more than a year, never saw him take his Violin from its case. Be it, however, as it may, death has not permitted the secret, of which Paganini spoke, to be divulged.

Many notices of the life and talent of this great artist have been published, either in collections or separately; the most important are the following:—

1. "Paganini's Leben und Treiben als Künstler und als Mensch," (Life and Adventures of Paganini, as an Artist, and

as a Man). Prague, Calve, 1830, in 8vo of 410 pages. This work, of which M. Schottky is the author, is but a compilation, without order, of correspondence, anecdotes, and German newspaper reports, as far as concerns the travels of the artist, from his first leaving Italy. An abridgment of this work, in which many doubtful facts and positive false accounts have been introduced, was published by M. L. Vinela, under the title of "Paganini's Leben und Charakter," (Life and Character of Paganini). Hamburg, Hoffmann and Campe, 1830, in 8vo.

2. "Paganini in seinem Reisewagen und Zimmer, in seinen redseligen Stunden, in gesellschaftlichen Zirkeln, und seinen Concerten," (Paganini in this Post-chaise, in his Room, in his hours of Privacy, in Society, and his Concerts). Brunswick, Vieweg, 1830, in 8vo of 68 pages. A work written in simplicity and good faith, indicating sound judgment. Mr. George Harrys, or Harris, the writer of this opusculum, was an Englishman, attached to the Court of Hanover. With a view of studying Paganini as a man and an artist, and to publish this notice, he became his interpreter and secretary, and remained with him an entire year.

3. "Leben, Character und Kunst N. Paganini's. Eine Skizze," (Sketch of the Life, Character, and Talent of Paganini, by M. F. C. J. Schütz, Professor at Halle). Leipzig, Rein, 1830, in 8vo.

4. "Notice sur le célèbre violoniste Nicolo Paganini," by M. J. Imbert de la Phalèque. Paris, E. Guyot, in 8vo, of 66 pages, with portrait.

5. "Paganini, his Life, his Person, and a few Words upon his Secret," by G. L. Anders. Paris, Delaunay, 1831, in 8vo.

6. "Paganini et Bériot, ou Avis aux artistes qui se destinent à l'enseignement du Violon," by Fr. Fayolle. Paris, Legouest, 1831, in 8vo.

7. "Vita di Nicolo Paganini di Genova, scritta ed illustrata da Giancarlo Conestabile, socio di varie Academie." Perugia, tipografia di Vincenzo Bartelli, 1831, 1 vol. in 8vo, 317 pages. An excellent work, carefully edited, and in a good spirit

of criticism, from documents chosen with discernment. The portrait of Paganini is given from M. Schottky's, but softened and idealized.

Independently of the portraits which accompany most of the above works, many were published in Italy, in Germany, and in France. The most sought for are the following:—1st. Portrait of Paganini, lithographed by Maurin, in the 7th volume of the Revue Musicale; 2nd, one lithographed by Mauzaise, in 4to, Paris, Bénard; 3rd, Milan, Ricordi; 4th, drawn and lithographed by Begas, Berlin, Sachse, in 4to; 5th, without name of author, in 4to, Berlin, Trautwein and Co.; 6th, drawn by Hahn, Munich, Falter; 7th, lithographed by Krätzschmar, Leipzig, Breitkopf and Härtel; 8th, without name of author, Vienna, Artaria, 1828; 9th, ditto, Hamburg, Niemeyer; 10th, ditto, Leipzig, Pönicke; 11th, ditto, Mannheim, Heckel.

Paganini Appreciated as a Composer.

ANALYSIS OF HIS WORKS.

LONG ere the talent of Paganini had acquired popularity beyond Italy, a collection of studies for the Violin, under his name, still unknown to French violinists, had been published, and created a deep impression; so many novelties were there accumulated, and the difficulties they presented were so problematical, and under forms so peculiar, that many professors doubted the possibility of their execution, and went so far as to look upon the publication of that work as a mystification. However, the composer, Andreozzi, who had brought to Paris the copy from which Pacini published his edition, attested that there was in Italy a man who executed those difficulties as though they were mere trifles, and who would astound the professors and pupils of the Conservatoire, if they heard him. This man was the author himself—it was Paganini.

At the same time, Blangini, on his return from Italy, also spoke of this artist with enthusiasm, and likewise attested that his art bore no affinity with the manner of playing the Violin that all great masters had propagated until his day; that all was the invention of his talent, and that he was destined to revolutionize the style of playing the Violin. Some young artists, among whom was Habeneck, attempted to solve these musical enigmas, but finally abandoned them, as they could not discover the application of these novelties to the pure music of the great composers.

The struggle between Lafont and Paganini resuscitated the confused recollection of his name, and the prodigies he effected were the subject of serious conversation. Insensibly the fact of his success became patent—the journals confirmed it, and the name of the artist gradually acquired popularity. However, fame blazoned forth his name as a violinist only—not as a composer. The twenty-four studies of the first work were only known in France, more than twenty years after it was published. It was only after he had enchanted all Paris, and had traversed France, gaining triumphs wherever he played, that the value of his compositions attracted some attention. They were then sought after. Italy and Germany were written to for copies of his concertos, his fantasias, and his airs with variations, but none of them had been published. The list of this artist's works which appeared, comprised the following only:—

1. "Ventiquattro Capricci per Violino solo, dedicati agli artisti, Op. 1." These studies or capriccios, in various keys, consist of arpeggi, staccati, trills in octaves, and scales in octaves, tenths, combinations of double, triple, and quadruple chords, etc.

2. "Sei Sonate per Violino e Chitarra, dedicati al Signor delle Piane." Op. 2.

3. "Sei Sonati per Violino e Chitarra, dedicati alla Ragazza Eleonora." Op. 3.

4. "Tre gran Quartetti a Violino, Viola, Chitarra e Violoncello, dedicati alle amatrici." Op. 4, Idem. Op. 5, Ibid. Paganini said of this work to Mr. Harrys, that it was not his, but was formed from some of his themes badly arranged.

These are the only positive productions of Paganini published up to the present day (June, 1851); all that has appeared since must be considered as commercial trickeries, as extracts from the preceding works, or simply as fugitive recollections of some artists. Such are the following:—

"Variazioni di bravura per Violino sopra un tema originale, con accompagnamento di Chitarra o Piano." These variations are those which form the twenty-fourth capriccio (in A minor) of the first work.

"Trois airs variés pour le Violon, pour être exécutés sur la quatrième corde seulement, avec accompagnement de Piano, par Gustave Carulli." These are recollections arranged by the author of the accompaniment.

"Introduzione e variazioni in sol sul tema, 'Nel cor più non mi sento' per Violino solo." This piece, published in the work of Guhr, upon the art of Paganini* is noted nearly from memory.

"Merveille de Paganini, ou duo pour le Violon seul en ut." This is also from Guhr.

Ghys published at Paris and at Berlin the "Carnaval de Venise, tel que le jouait Paganini." Ernst and Sivori have also given, as exact traditions of this musical pleasantry, versions differing more or less, which gave rise to discussions in the newspapers. The publication of the veritable "Carnaval de Venise" of the illustrious violinist will remove all uncertainty in this respect.

Paganini was aware that the interest which his concerts created would diminish materially, if he published the compositions he performed. He resolved therefore upon not publishing them until after he had ceased to travel, and had retired from his career of executive artist. He only carried with him the orchestral parts of those pieces he habitually played; and no one ever saw the Violin solo parts of these compositions, for he dreaded the indiscretion of all who sought to gain access to him. He seldom spoke of his works, even to his most intimate friends, consequently an indistinct notion of the nature and number of these works could alone exist. M. Conestabile, who made every effort to acquire the truth of all that concerned the person, the talent, and the success of Paganini, has published in his book the catalogue which was sent to him of all the manuscript and original works of Paganini preserved by his son.

The titles of the works are as follows :—

1. Four Concertos for the Violin, with accompaniments.

2. Four other concertos, the orchestral parts unwritten. The last was written a short time prior to his death, at Nice.

* Published by Schott & Co., Mayence and London.

3. Variations upon a comic theme continued for the orchestra.

4. Sonata for the large Viol, with orchestral parts.

5. "God save the King," varied for the Violin, with orchestral parts.

6. "Le Streghe," variations on a ballet air, with orchestral parts.

7. Variations upon "Non più mesta," theme from "Cenerentola."

8. Grand Sentimental Sonata.

9. Sonata, with variations.

10. "La Primavera," (Spring), Sonata, without accompaniments.

11. "Varsovie," Sonata.

12. La ci darem la mano.

13. "Le Carnaval de Venise."

14. "Di tanti palpiti."

15. "Marie Louise."

16. Romance pour le chant.

17. Cantabile for Violin and Piano.

18. Polonaise, with variations.

19. Fantaisie Vocale.

20. Sonata, for Violin Solo.

21. Nine Quartetts, for Violin, Alto, Violoncello, and Guitar.

22. Cantabile and Waltz.

23. Three Duetts, for Violin and Violoncello.

24. Other Duetts and small Pieces for Violin and Guitar.

Unfortunately many of these compositions are incomplete. The original scores, without omissions, which have been found, are the two concertos in E flat and in B minor (it is in this latter the celebrated rondo of "La Clochette" is found); the allegro of a sonata, entitled "Movimento perpetuo"; the famous variations "Le Streghe" (the Witches) with orchestral parts; the variations upon "God save the King," with parts; variations upon "Di tanti palpiti," with parts; variations upon "Non più mesta, accanto al fuoco," with parts; the "Carnaval de Venise," twenty-four variations upon a popular Venetian air; and sixty variations, in three series, with accompaniment for Piano or

Guitar, upon the popular air known at Genoa under the name of "Barucaba." The theme is very short; the variations are studies of various kind of difficulties. These were written by Paganini, at Genoa, in February, 1835, and were among his latest works; he dedicated them to his friend the advocate, M. L. G. Germi. By some singular circumstance these variations are not included in the list furnished by M. Conestabile.

It will be seen the complete works of Paganini, which have been found, are only nine in number. It is to be deplored that among these high-class productions, the magnificent concerto that the great artist wrote for Paris, and which he played at his third concert at the opera, the 25th of March 1831, should be wanting; also the grand military sonata upon the fourth string in which he displayed such marvellous ability, in a compass of three octaves with harmonic sounds; and, finally, his variations upon "Nel cor più non mi sento."

The compositions of Paganini are redolent with merit—novelty in ideas, elegance of form, richness of harmony, and variety in the effects of instrumentation. These qualities are especially found in his concertos, which have exercised great influence on compositions of this nature that have subsequently been published. They differ in form in many points from the classic form of Viotti's concertos. There is the merit of uniformity and increasing interest, which it were well all violinists would meditate upon. In general, without diverting attention from the solo by over-elaborated passages, the instrumentation possessed an interest which cannot be separated from the principal design. The *entrées* are neither cold nor symmetrical—the effects new and varied.

The first concerto is in E flat, set for the orchestra, but the Violin are written in D; the four strings of the instrument are consequently tuned a semitone higher. The tutti, admirably written, is bold and flowing, and very effective. The forms remind one generally of those of the old concerto, more than of those Paganini wrote since, this being his first. I have an indistinct recollection of his having composed this one in 1811. There is little originality in the style of the tutti and the solos; but in the details, and above all, in the brilliant passages, there are certain points which render this concerto a work of the greatest interest; there is frequent employment of double notes and harmonics. The second solo presents effects on the fourth string, of which effects Paganini is the inventor. It terminates with the last passage of the first solo transposed into the original key.

The adagio (in C minor) is a dialogue between the fourth string and the other three. The conception of this dialogue appears to have absorbed all the artist's attention, for the melody has little novelty. This is not the case with the rondo—the theme of which is peculiarly original. There is an extraordinary staccato passage, which Paganini executed in a novel manner, peculiar to himself. It is necessary to understand the method to give this passage its original character. It is in this rondo that Paganini employed, for the first time, tenths, combined in various ways, producing wonderful effects, by the unerring and marvellous certainty of his mechanism. The character of the piece is bold: the second solo, nearly all on the fourth string and in harmonics, produced an extraordinary sensation, nothing similar having been heard prior to its introduction.

The second concerto is in B minor. The commencement of the first piece is broad and impassioned; the harmony often interesting in its successions; the instrumentation intelligent and rich in effects. The tutti are weak in development, and serve only to connect together the various solo parts. The phrase of the commencement of the first solo is very grand, and largely developed, followed by a modulation in D, where much boldness is displayed in a novel passage of double notes. The melody which follows is somewhat poor—the four first bars being repeated without any change—which is a fault; but the passage which follows is particularly effective. Paganini in this has evinced much daring in the combination of difficulties, both for the bow and the left hand. He has introduced a double shake, descending in thirds—in the execution of which he was incomparable, both in brilliancy and the irreproachable perfection of his intonation.

The second tutti, which recalls the subject of the first, is rather short, but interesting; it modulates in E minor, and terminates with an unusual form of suspension. The subject of the second solo differs totally from the first; the melody is expressive and combines effects of staccato, to which Paganini imparted a character quite peculiar. The passage which follows this subject, all in double notes, is very effective: its combinations present immense difficulties, which to the great artist were but mere trifles. The second solo ends in B major, finishes with the passage of the first, transposed into this new key, and consequently rendered much more difficult.

Throughout this first piece, the double-note passages and jumping bowing are quite novel, and depart entirely from the ordinary form of the concerto. Two things are equally remarkable in the manner Paganini played them. The first was his perfect intonation of the double notes in this shoal of difficulties, particularly in the excessive rapidity in the passages; the second was the marvellous skill with which he managed the bow, however great the distances of the intervals. There was in this part alone of the artist's talent an evident predestination, and the study of an entire life. It is impossible to give any idea of all the combinations which are met in the fingering of the chords strewn among these immensely difficult passages; they embrace occasionally such extraordinary intervals, that violinists are at a loss to discover the artifices by which the hand reaches them. Besides, in this labyrinth of unheard-of difficulties, neither a doubtful note nor uncertain intonation ever occurred.

The adagio (in D) is a cantabile of the finest character. More simple than the rest of Paganini's compositions, it produced but little effect, finishing as it does without the exhibition of extraordinary difficulties, which the public were wont to expect from him; nevertheless, the forms of the melody are elegant, expressive, and full of charms. Good taste prevails throughout this piece. The rondo with the obbligato bell accompaniment is delightfully fanciful; the most incomprehensible feats of skill are here combined with exquisite taste. The first subject is remarkable for its elegance and novelty, both in its details and its general formation. Some charming bow effects are introduced, which Paganini executed with marvellous brilliancy and dexterity. The bow fluttered so nimbly over the strings, and the fingers moved so briskly and lightly, that the performance seemed one of easy accomplishment. The rondo of the "Clochette" obtained enthusiastic success throughout Europe.

The allegro of the sonata for Violin and orchestra, entitled "Movimento perpetuo," is only remarkable as a study for detached bowing of exceedingly rapid movement, which continues until the last bar. This species of difficulty exacts great suppleness of arm to avoid fatigue, and a perfect *ensemble* of the left hand and the bow. In this piece there are no less than 170 bars without a single rest. Considered as a composition, it is unimportant, but interesting as a study.

Few musical compositions ever obtained such universal fame as the "Streghe" (the Witches), either from the prodigious execution of the great violinist, or perhaps because some superstition attached to the title. The original manuscript indicates that the introduction and the variations are composed upon an original air; however, if tradition is to be depended upon, the air was taken from the ballet of "Il Noce di Benevento." The introduction is short. The first variation, in double and triple notes, is extremely difficult. It may be regarded as a valuable study for playing in tune. In the second there is a mixture of harmonics and pizzicato which produces a very original effect. The third is a dialogue between the fourth string and the double harmonics; a novel effect which never failed to draw down the loudest acclamations of the auditory. The finale, which joins this variation, terminates with rapid passages upon the fourth string, and in harmonics of extreme difficulty.

In the variations upon "God save the King," Paganini seems to have intended concentrating all the new effects he had discovered, and all the enormous difficulties over which he had triumphed. The subject is written in three and in four parts; the melody is played with the bow, and the other parts of the accompaniment is pizzicato. The first variation, in double notes, presents successions of thirds and tenths, which require a large hand and a great certainty of intonation. Paganini played it in a light and rapid manner, which greatly increased its difficulty. The second variation is a complication of rapid triplets, intermingled with passages of double notes and bounding staccatos. The execution of this variation requires extraordinary dexterity. In the third the subject is sustained in a slow movement, during which the accompaniment is going on in extremely rapid passages on the third and fourth strings. The fourth is peculiarly quaint; it consists in rapid passages pizzicato in the upper part, while the accompaniment is played upon the lower, with the bow staccato. The fifth, written in double notes, is an echo effect on the upper octave, the bass is by pizzicato on the lower strings. The sixth and last consists in staccato arpeggios, difficult of execution, arising from the complex positions of the left hand.

In the fantasia with variations, on "Di tanti palpiti," the orchestra is written in B flat, the solo a semitone higher; in the second variation the fourth string is lowered to B flat. Paganini effected this change with so much address, that it was never perceived at his concerts. The piece commences by an introductory larghetto, followed by a recitative. The subject which follows is quite simple, and the first variation without very remarkable difficulties, with the exception of a very rapid descending scale in harmonics. In the second, where the fourth string is lowered to B flat, passages occur in double notes of great difficulty for the bow. The third is the most curious and difficult; it consists of arpeggios with double notes in a presto movement, and combinations of harmonics and ordinary notes in a new and quaint style.

The air with variations, on "La Cenerentola" (Non più mesta), is written in E flat for the Orchestra; the Violin is tuned a semitone higher. The first variation contains nothing remarkable; the second, a combination of bounding staccato harmonics and pizzicato, recalls similar passages found in other works of the author. The third, in a minor mood, is composed nearly of octaves. The fourth is an echo, the effects are double harmonics. It is followed by a finale in thirds and octaves, brilliantly effective, but fraught with difficulty.

The twenty variations upon the popular air "Oh, Mamma," known as the "Carnaval de Venise," which has been so frequently imitated, is remarkable for the distinct character given to each; all the bow and finger effects imagined by Paganini are concentrated in it. Good taste is sometimes departed from in a few of the variations, but it will not be denied that some extraordinary effects are produced in those strange freaks, to which the marvellous dexterity of the artist lent an irresistible charm.

The last work to which I have to allude is the collection of sixty variations, in the form of studies, upon the popular air "Barucaba." Paganini purposed in each of these studies to give every style of bowing, all the difficulties of fingering, and all the combinations of harmony, upon which his school is founded. By a singular notion, nearly all these variations are written in different keys.

If the astonishing success of Paganini, the immense popularity of his name, and the influence he exercised over the talent of some of the violinists of the younger school, be considered, the high interest attached to the publication of the works with which the great artist astonished Europe, will be understood. At all events, these considerations will afford but a very imperfect idea of the importance of their long-withheld publication. Their value can only be understood after a long and close examination. For more than twenty years every violinist has looked forward to the production of these works with anxiety and curiosity, under the impression of being able, with them, to "do the Paganini," and establish himself, if not in imitation, at least as a pupil of that illustrious man. But few imagined the great truths which would manifest themselves by the revelation of the secret of his music —none could foresee how much this great man would be elevated in their esteem when the prodigious difficulties he executed while playing, were placed before them. Some of his effects, the most easy of execution, were hastily copied, and the mystery of his talent was supposed to have been discovered. How much illusion will be dissipated by the examination and study of these anxiously expected works! I will not speak of the simply curious effects by which Paganini dazzled the million—of his pizzicato and bow feats—of the modifications in tuning the instrument, and of the thousand combinations, the merit of which consisted principally in perfect execution. These will only have an exceptional existence, and will never hold a place in serious music. Besides, the sagacity of Guhr, a skilful violinist, and the able conductor of the Frankfort Theatre, has penetrated, to a certain extent, the secret of these things, and has cleverly exposed the theory in a work especially devoted to this purpose.* That which most struck me on reading the MSS. of Paganini, that which raised him immensely in my estimation, was the conviction that the mechanism of the art was never carried to the same extent—that he was never equalled in surmounting difficulties—and never was such infinite variety displayed in brilliant passages. The double notes for instance, always the test of great Violinists, as respects true intonation and precision—particularly when the left hand descends to it natural position—form a salient feature in the rapid passages of his compositions. The intervals are ever varying—sometimes in thirds, sometimes in sixths, eighths, and tenths—passing with rapidity from one kind of interval to another—jumping incredible distances—always in double notes—with unerring certainty and perfect intonation. His hand was a geometrical compass which divided the finger board with mathematical precision—his fingers falling exactly where the intonation of the intervals of the double notes was to be found. I do not speak of the varieties of bowing, by which he rendered these difficulties more complicated, I merely look at the double-note passages alone,—I therefore say, that these passages, which were trifles to Paganini, will be impracticable to any other violinist

* "Essai sur l'art de jouer du Violon, de Paganini." Mayence e Londres, Schott & Co.

whomsoever he may be, if he would execute them with the same rapidity and with the perfect intonation of the author. As a study, it is a new world for the perseverance of young artists, the results of which will be the acquisition of certainty, which only a small number of performers possess, and the enlargement of the great resources of the instrument.

It may be asked why new difficulties are introduced into art; and it may be remarked, with reason, that the aim of music is not to surprise with marvellous feats, but to delight the feelings. This principle I perfectly coincide with; yet I would observe, on the one hand, that certain artists will never be prevented from endeavouring to overcome difficulties, however apparently insurmountable, nor the public from applauding the happy result of their efforts: on the other hand, that the study of difficulties conduces to certainty in what is more simple. If any violinist can play, with perfect intonation, and in the prescribed time, the passages of Paganini's concertos, he will necessarily attain imperturbable certainty in ordinary music.

Is it imperative, I may ask, that these new and varied forms of passages in Violin concertos are to be excluded? Admirable in sentiment, as avowedly the concertos of Viotti are, their weakness consists in the monotony of the rapid passages—and the same may be said of nearly all other known concertos. Art is evidently limited in this species of composition, to things which cannot be considered as the last essay of the artist's skill—more may be boldly attempted, and that by varied means. Let the happy darings of Paganini be studied, and it will be found that something is gained.